CLASSROOM MANAGEMENT FOR SECONDARY TEACHERS

CLASSROOM MANAGEMENT FOR SECONDARY TEACHERS

EDMUND T. EMMER
Research and Development Center for Teacher Education,
University of Texas at Austin

CAROLYN M. EVERTSON
Instructional Systems, Inc.,
Vandervoort, Arkansas

JULIE P. SANFORD
Research and Development Center for Teacher Education,
University of Texas at Austin

BARBARA S. CLEMENTS
Research and Development Center for Teacher Education,
University of Texas at Austin

MURRAY E. WORSHAM
Northeast Independent School District,
San Antonio, Texas

PRENTICE-HALL, INC., Englewood Cliffs, New Jersey 07632

Library of Congress Cataloging in Publication Data
Main entry under title:
Classroom management for secondary teachers.
  Bibliography: p. 165
  Includes index.
  1. Classroom management—Case studies. 2. Education,
Secondary—Case studies. I. Emmer, Edmund T.
LB3013.C53 1984   373.11′02   83-11156
ISBN 0-13-136150-3
ISBN 0-13-136143-0 (pbk.)

Editorial/production supervision
  and interior design: Kate Kelly
Cover design: Wanda Lubelska Design
Manufacturing buyer: Ron Chapman

Printed in the United States of America

10 9 8 7 6 5 4 3 2 1

ISBN 0-13-136150-3
ISBN 0-13-136143-0 {PBK}

Prentice-Hall International, Inc., *London*
Prentice-Hall of Australia Pty. Limited, *Sydney*
Editora Prentice-Hall do Brasil, Ltda., *Rio de Janeiro*
Prentice-Hall Canada Inc., *Toronto*
Prentice-Hall of India Private Limited, *New Delhi*
Prentice-Hall of Japan, Inc., *Tokyo*
Prentice-Hall of Southeast Asia Pte. Ltd., *Singapore*
Whitehall Books Limited, *Wellington, New Zealand*

CONTENTS

CHAPTER TWO
CHOOSING RULES AND PROCEDURES √   **15**

CHAPTER THREE
MANAGING STUDENT WORK √   **39**

CHAPTER FOUR
REWARDS AND PENALTIES   ✓   **55**

CHAPTER FIVE
GETTING OFF TO A GOOD START   69

CHAPTER SIX
MAINTAINING GOOD STUDENT BEHAVIOR   93

CHAPTER SEVEN
ORGANIZING AND CONDUCTING INSTRUCTION   109

CHAPTER EIGHT
MANAGING SPECIAL GROUPS   **127**

CHAPTER NINE
EVALUATING YOUR CLASSROOM'S ORGANIZATION
AND MANAGEMENT   **147**

PREFACE

Good classroom management doesn't just happen. Smoothly running classrooms whose students are highly involved in learning activities and which are free from disruption and chronic misbehavior are not accidental. They exist because effective teachers have a very clear idea of the types of classroom conditions and student behaviors that are needed for good learning environments, and because those teachers work very hard to produce such behaviors and conditions. This book describes what *you* can do to create a well-managed classroom. The process is described as teachers encounter it: first, planning in several key areas before the school year begins; next, implementing the plan and establishing good management at the beginning of the year; and finally, maintaining the management procedures throughout the year. We have tried to make the materials as useful and practical to you as possible by providing checklists to help organize your planning activities in key areas. Numerous case studies are also provided to illustrate how important concepts can be applied in classrooms. All the case studies have been based on observations in junior and senior high school classrooms, with changes in names and other identifying characteristics of classes. We hope you will find much here that is helpful to you as your plan and organize your own classroom.

As teachers, our own experiences have influenced our understanding of classrooms. However, most of our knowledge about classroom management has been derived from research in over 300 elementary and secondary classrooms. Most of these classes were observed both at the beginning of and throughout the school year. The goal was to identify management practices associated with high levels of student engagement in learning activities and low levels of disruptive behavior, two classroom conditions that contribute to good student achievement. Data collected in classes taught by effective teachers, as identified in these classroom management studies, were the main source of the guidelines, suggestions, and case studies in this book. The research program was conducted over a five-year period at the Research and Development Center for Teacher Education, University of Texas, and it was supported by the National Institute of Education. Of course, the views expressed in this book are those of the authors and not the official positions of the Center or of the Institute.

We would like to acknowledge our large debt of gratitude to the teachers who permitted us to observe in their classrooms. Without the base of reality they provided, this book would not exist. We are also grateful to the many observers, school administrators, and other researchers who both assisted and enlightened us. Finally, we are very grateful for the skills of Judy Camps and Kitty Hays, who typed this manuscript.

CLASSROOM MANAGEMENT FOR SECONDARY TEACHERS

CHAPTER ONE
ORGANIZING
YOUR CLASSROOM
AND MATERIALS

A logical starting point for classroom management is arranging the physical setting for teaching. This includes classroom space, furniture, equipment, and supplies. This is a logical starting point because it is a task that you must complete before the school year begins. Many teachers find it easier to plan other aspects of classroom management after they have a clear idea of how the physical features of their classroom will be organized.

Good room arrangement is important for classroom management because it can help you cope with the complex demands of teaching twenty-five to thirty students at a time for five or more periods a day. During any given period students will come and go, many activities will occur, and you and your class will use a variety of materials, texts, reference books, equipment, and supplies. Appropriate room preparation and arrangement of materials conserve class time for learning, while inadequate planning interferes with instruction by causing interruptions, delays, and dead time.

When you arrange the classroom, you will need to make many decisions. Should desks be set out in rows? Where should your desk be located? What areas of the room will you use for presentations? How will you and the students obtain materials and supplies, and where will these be stored? This chapter will help you make these and other decisions about room arrangement. Each component will be described along with guidelines and examples to help you plan. In addition, a checklist for organizing your classroom, supplies, and equipment is provided. Use it to focus your efforts and to be certain that your classroom is ready for the beginning of school.

FOUR KEYS TO GOOD ROOM ARRANGEMENT

Remember that the classroom is the workspace for both you and your students. While it may hold as many as thirty students each period, it is not a very large area. Your students will be participating in a variety of activities and using different areas of the room, and they will need to enter and leave the room rapidly when classes change. You will get better results if you arrange your room to permit orderly movement, few distractions, and efficient use of available space. The following four keys will be helpful as guidelines when you make decisions about arranging your room.

Keep high traffic areas free of congestion. High traffic areas include group work areas, the space around the pencil sharpener and trash can, doorways, certain bookshelves and supply areas, student desks, and the teacher's desk. High traffic areas should be kept away from each other, have plenty of space, and be easily accessible.

Be sure students are easily seen by the teacher. Careful monitoring of students is a major management task. If the teacher cannot see students, it will be difficult to prevent task avoidance or disruption. Therefore, clear lines of sight must be maintained between areas of the room that the teacher will frequent and student work areas.

Keep frequently used teaching materials and student supplies readily accessible. Easy access to and efficient storage of such materials and supplies will aid classroom management by allowing activities to begin and end promptly and by minimizing time spent getting ready and cleaning up.

Be certain students can easily see instructional presentations and displays. Be sure that the seating arrangements will allow students to see the overhead projector screen or chalkboard without moving their chairs, turning their desks around, or craning their necks. Don't put your

THE FIRST DAY OF SCHOOL!! IT ALL SEEMS SO HOPELESS! —NEXT SUMMER IS JUST A SHIMMERING MIRAGE ON THE DESERT HORIZON!!

COME ON, SKYLER... IT CAN'T BE ALL THAT TERRIBLE.

DO YOU HAVE ANY IDEA HOW LONG IT TAKES TO BREAK IN A NEW TEACHER?

Reprinted by permission of Tribune Company Syndicate, Inc.

instructional area in a far corner of the room, away from a substantial number of students. Such conditions do not encourage students to pay attention, and they make it more difficult for students to take notes or copy material.

Each of the four keys presented above will help accomplish good room arrangement. Some specific suggestions for achieving this goal are described below. By attending to these areas, you will address all the important aspects of room preparation. You can then be confident that you will have designed a physical setting that is conducive to student involvement.

SUGGESTIONS FOR ARRANGING YOUR CLASSROOM

Bulletin Boards and Walls

Wall space and bulletin boards provide areas to display student work, instructionally relevant material, decorative items, assignments, rules, schedules, a clock, and other items of interest. Ceiling space can also be used to hang mobiles and other decorations. The following points should be considered when preparing these areas.

1. At the start of school, you should have at least the following displays for walls and chalkboards: a place for listing daily assignments, and some decorative display to catch your students' interest, such as a bulletin board with a "Welcome Back to School" motif or a display organized around a school-spirit theme ("Go Hippos!").

2. If you are teaching at the junior high level, or if you are teaching ninth graders in a senior high school, you should also reserve some wall or bulletin board space for posting classroom rules (at higher grade levels you might also post rules, or you might handle the communication of expectations orally and/or via a handout—see Chapters Two and Five).

3.   Other displays that many teachers find useful include an example of the correct paper heading to be used in your class, and a content-relevant display such as one highlighting a topic that will soon be taught.

4.   Covering large bulletin board areas with colored paper is an easy way to brighten your classroom. This paper comes on large rolls and is often kept in the school office or in a supply room. You can also trim the bulletin boards with an edging or border of corrugated paper. If you can't find these items in your supply room, consider spending a few dollars for these materials at a school supply center or variety store. You can also find books of bulletin board ideas as well as posters, cardboard punch-out letters, stencils, and other graphics for sale at such stores.

5.   If you need ideas for decorating your room or for setting up displays, borrow some from other teachers. A look in some other rooms will probably give you several new ideas. Also, your departmental supply room may contain some instructionally relevant display material. Ask your department chairperson for assistance, if necessary.

6.   Don't spend a lot of time decorating your room. You will have many other, more important things to do to get ready for the beginning of school. A few bare bulletin boards won't bother anybody. Leave one or two empty; you can add displays later or allow your homeroom/advisory students to decorate a blank space for an art project. You can also reward a "class of the month" with the privilege of redecorating a bulletin board. Finally, don't overdecorate your classroom. Wall space that's too filled up with detail can be distracting to the students; also, it makes a room seem smaller. It will seem small enough when twenty-five to thirty students are in it.

Floor Space

Arrange your furniture and equipment so that you can easily observe students from all areas of the room in which you will work. Students should be able to see you as well as the overhead projector screen, the main chalkboard, and any other area that will be used for making presentations to the whole class. Of course, you will have to adjust to whatever constraints exist in your assigned classroom. A classroom may be too small or have inadequate or poorly located chalkboard space or electrical outlets. You should assess your space and determine whether any changes can be made to accommodate whatever constraints exist. For example, if the classroom is small, be sure to remove unnecessary student desks or extra furniture or equipment; if you have inadequate storage, perhaps you can locate an extra file or supply cabinet.

A good starting point for your floor plan is to locate where you will conduct whole-class instruction. Examine the room and identify where you will stand or work when you address the entire class to conduct lessons or give instructions. You can usually identify this area of the room by the location of a large chalkboard and the placement of the overhead projector screen. This area should also have space for a table or desk where you can place items needed in presentations and an electrical out-

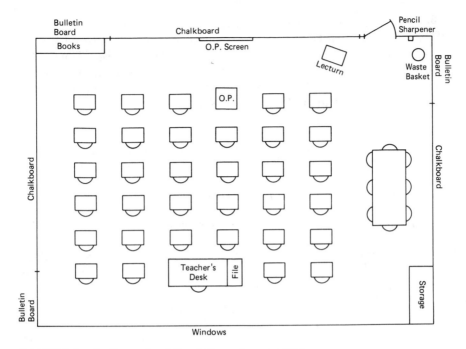

FIGURE 1-1. An Example of Good Room Arrangement

let for the overhead projector. Once you have located this area, you are ready to begin planning floor space.

As you read each item below, you should refer to Figure 1-1, which shows a well designed floor plan for a secondary school classroom. Note how each item is addressed in this floor plan. Of course, this is just one of many possibilities. The location of desks, work areas, and other physical features of the classroom depend on the size and shape of the room and how different parts of the room will be used.

1. Arrangement of student desks.   Many different arrangements of student desks are possible, but be sure to arrange them so that all students can look at the whole-group instruction area without having to get out of their seats. Also avoid having students sit with their backs to the area. Try to avoid having students face potential sources of distraction such as windows, the doorway, an area where small groups of students will work, or eye-catching displays. *Even if other arrangements are to be used later in the year, you might start the year with desks in rows facing the major instructional area.* In such an arrangement students are less likely to distract each other than they would be if their desks were arranged in groups with students facing one another. In the example presented in Figure 1-1, the desks are arranged in rows, and no student is seated with his or her back to the major instructional area. Thus, if the teacher puts a display on the overhead projector screen, all the students can see it easily. This allows them the opportunity to copy material from the screen while sitting at their desks. The following items may also be of concern.

Since it is important to keep high traffic areas clear, don't put desks or other furniture in front of doors, the pencil sharpener, sinks, and so on.

Be sure to leave ample room around student desks so that you can easily approach students when you are monitoring seatwork activities.

Count the desks or chairs and make sure you have enough.

Replace damaged furniture or have it repaired.

2. The teacher's desk, filing cabinet, overhead projector, and other equipment.   Your desk needs to be placed where it is functional. If you intend to keep at your desk instructional materials used during presentations, the desk should be adjacent to the main instructional area or areas. If you plan to work at your desk at any time during the day, you will need to locate your desk so as to facilitate monitoring: Sit facing the students and be sure you can observe all of them from your seat. However, it is not necessary that students be able to see you from their seats, and some teachers prefer placing their desks at the back of the room rather than at the front. If you plan to work with individual students at your desk, you will also have to consider traffic patterns near your desk. Student desks should not be so close to yours that students will be distracted by other students approaching your desk or working with you there.

Other furniture items, such as the filing cabinet and storage bins, need to be located where they are functional. An item used for storing seldom-used supplies can be safely tucked away in a corner or hidden out of view. Furniture that contains items that will be used frequently during class should be located near the area in which they will be used. All electrical equipment must, of course, be placed near an outlet.

3. Bookcases.   These should be placed where they will neither prevent your monitoring students nor obstruct students' ability to see chalkboards or relevant displays. If a bookcase contains items that are to be used frequently, such as dictionaries or supplemental readers, it needs to be conveniently located and easily monitored. If a bookcase is used to store seldom-used items, an out-of-the-way place is best. If you have only one bookcase, store unneeded items in a cabinet so that the single bookcase can be used for materials in frequent use.

4. Work areas.   In many subjects, such as science, industrial arts, homemaking, or art, students may spend part of their time in a laboratory, shop, or other work area. The area may be in the same room or in another room adjacent to the classroom. Students may work individually or in groups. Students may also work in small groups for discussion activities or for special projects in other subject areas as well. When arranging group work or laboratory areas, follow the same principles you used when positioning student desks. Be sure you can see all students, keep traffic lanes clear, and avoid congested areas, especially near supply and cleanup areas. Provide clear lines of sight between students and any area of the room from which you will conduct instruction while students are in the work area.

5. Centers.   A center is an area where a few students come to work on a special activity or to study some topic. Often a center will have special equipment, such as a tape recorder with headphones, for individual students. Other centers may be organized around a special study topic or around skill areas in a particular subject. In the latter case, the teacher might have a box of activity cards that students use to progress through a series of objectives as part of enrichment or remediation programs. It is important to note that you do not need to have a center in your room, particularly at the beginning of the school year. There will be time enough later to introduce this feature into your classes if you so desire. If and when you do use a center, be sure to place it in a location where you can monitor students easily. Also, be certain that all necessary materials and equipment are available at the center and work properly.

6. Pets, plants, aquariums, and special items.   These can add interest and individuality to a room. However, the first week of school is already quite exciting for students, so it isn't necessary to introduce these special features immediately. When you do bring in such items, place them where they won't be distracting, especially during whole-class activities. Of course, they should not impede movement about the room nor interfere with students' work activities.

Storage Space and Supplies

Once you have decided on your wall and bulletin board displays and have organized space within the classroom, you can concentrate on obtaining supplies and providing for storage. Some supplies will be used frequently and thus will need to be readily accessible. Other items will be seasonal or infrequently used and can go into deeper storage.

1. Textbooks and other instructional materials.   You need to identify the textbooks and supplemental materials (dictionaries, reference books, supplemental reading materials) that will be used in your class. Determine which books the students are expected to keep in their possession and which must remain in the room. Then find easily accessible shelves in a bookcase for those everyday books and materials that will not be kept by students. If you don't know what supplemental materials are available or what the school policies are regarding these items, check with your department chairperson, with the librarian, or with another teacher. Also, find out what system is used for obtaining textbooks; often it is first come, first served. If so, get in line early to ensure that you obtain the books you need.

2. Frequently used classroom materials.   These are supplies that you and your students will use; and the necessary items will depend somewhat on the subject you teach. A basic set includes paper in varying sizes and colors, water-soluble markers, rulers, scissors, chalk and erasers, transparent tape and masking tape, stapler, and glue. Other than the chalk kept in the chalk trays, these and any other supplies you need on a daily basis should be kept in a readily accessible place, such as on a worktable or shelf. Usually students are expected to supply certain materials, including pencils, erasers, pens, and notebook paper or spiral notebooks. Since you cannot expect that all students will bring these materials at the beginning of the year, you should make sure you have an ample supply of items needed by students. It is also a good idea to give parents a list of supplies that their children will need in your class.

3. Teacher's supplies.   You will receive some materials from the school office for your own use. These items, which usually should be stored in your desk, include pencils and pens, paper, extra chalk, overhead transparency sheets, scissors, ruler, stapler, file folders, paper clips, and thumbtacks. In addition, you should receive a grade book, a lesson plan book, teachers' editions for all textbooks, and any forms or tablets needed for attendance reports and for handling money. Set up a filing system that allows you to separate the notes, forms, papers, and other materials used in each class. Use different file folders for different periods. For each period, keep frequently needed materials and forms separate from those needed only occasionally.

4. Other materials.   In addition to the items supplied by the school, a number of other supplies will come in handy. If your room does not have a clock and a calendar, obtain these now. Both should be large enough to be seen from all areas of the room. You may wish to buy a desk bell or a timer if you are going to use these as signals for starting or stopping activities. You might also add the following items: kleenex, rags or paper towels, a bar of soap, bandages, and scouring powder or liquid cleanser. Some teachers like to keep a few basic tools such as a hammer, pliers, and screwdriver in case a minor repair needs to be made. Store all these items where they are accessible to you but not to your students.

5. *Equipment.*   Check all equipment, including the overhead projector, record player, tape recorder, headphones, pencil sharpener, and so on, to make sure they are in working order. Get any necessary extension cords or adapter plugs and store these either with the equipment or in a handy place.

6. *Seasonal or infrequently used items.*   This category includes Halloween, Thanksgiving, and Christmas items as well as other seasonal decorations, bulletin board displays, or special project materials. Also included are instructional materials that are used only on some occasions; for example, compasses and protractors, templates, special art materials, science equipment, and so on. Because you don't need to have ready access to these materials, you can store them at the back of closets, in boxes on top of cabinets, or even out of the room, if you have access to outside storage space. Check with your department chairperson about using a storeroom.

"Come now, Miss Twist,
your class isn't *that* large!"

7. Special project materials.   In a few subject areas, such as industrial arts, homemaking, or art, students may regularly work on projects. Occasionally these projects may produce objects that are bulky or awkward to store in lockers and which must thus remain in the room. You will need to provide special storage areas to which you can control access in order to safeguard the materials. You'll be wise to avoid beginning such projects until you have arranged for adequate storage.

IF YOU HAVE TO FLOAT

At some time in their careers, many teachers have to share classrooms with other teachers. Sometimes teachers who are new to a school find that they have no classroom that they can call their own but instead have to "float," conducting their classes in three or more rooms during the day. Obviously, such a situation presents some problems for classroom organization and management. If this is the situation you face, your ability to arrange and organize your classroom space the way you would like will be very limited. However, there are some things you can and should do before school begins.

First, confer with the other teachers whose classrooms you will be using. Inspect each room carefully so that you will know where everything is when school begins. In each room try to arrange for the following:

An overhead projector in place for daily use. This is practically a must. You will not have the time—and you may not have the space—to put lessons, assignments, notices, and so on, on the chalkboards each period. You can save yourself much effort by preparing ahead of time transparencies to use in each of your classes. Also, you can use blank transparency sheets to write on as you would a chalkboard during lesson presentations. (Another advantage of using transparencies instead of chalkboards in borrowed classrooms is that they provide you with a record of what you presented to your students.)

A regular space on the chalkboard or on a bulletin board where you can post assignments or announcements for your class and leave them up for a week or more.

One shelf, cabinet, or table, especially if your course requires a classroom set of materials that you cannot carry around with you all day.

A sufficient number of desks.

Either plan to carry all essential teaching supplies with you each day or store them in one desk drawer or in a box in each room. Don't depend on other teachers for supplies. You will definitely need plenty of transparency sheets, transparency markers, chalk, extra pens and pencils, paper, paper clips, and kleenex. File folders, large manilla envelopes, and rubber bands will be useful for organizing and carrying student papers.

CHECKLIST 1: ROOM ARRANGEMENT

To organize and keep track of your activities as you arrange your room and get supplies and equipment ready, you will find it helpful to use Checklist 1. Each aspect of room arrangement has been listed, and space has been provided for noting things to be done and for checking off the area, once you have it ready.

CHECKLIST 1   Room Preparation

Subject	Check When Complete	Notes
A. Bulletin Boards and Walls	_____	
B. Floor Space		
1. Student desks/tables	_____	
2. Teacher's desk and equipment	_____	
3. Bookcases	_____	
4. Work areas	_____	
5. Centers	_____	
6. Pets and plants		
C. Storage Space and Supplies		
1. Textbooks	_____	
2. Frequently used instructional materials	_____	
3. Teacher's supplies	_____	
4. Other materials	_____	
5. Equipment	_____	
6. Seasonal items	_____	
7. Special project materials	_____	

SUGGESTED ACTIVITIES

The activities described below will help you plan and organize your classroom space. Do as many of them as you have time for.

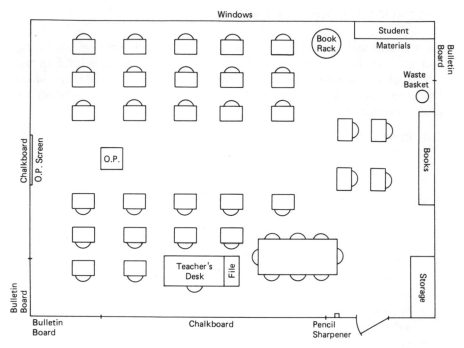

FIGURE 1-2.   A Room Arrangement with Problems

1.   The drawing in Figure 1-2 shows how one teacher arranged her classroom. There are quite a few problems with this room arrangement. See how many you can find, and consider how each problem might be corrected. (A key for this activity is in Appendix B.)

2.   Make a scale drawing of your room, as in Figures 1-1 and 1-2. You can now experiment on paper with different furniture arrangements and the organization of space—a much simpler task than pushing the furniture around yourself. Try to evaluate your arrangement, using the four keys to successful room arrangement presented earlier in the chapter.

3.   Visit some other teachers' classrooms and examine their room arrangements. Use the items in Checklist 1 and the four keys to room arrangement to guide your observation and analysis. If you are having a specific problem, ask several teachers for suggestions and see how they may have coped with the same problem.

4.   After you have arranged your furniture in your room, test the traffic patterns, keeping in mind the recommendations in this chapter.

a.   Go to each instructional area and check it for your ability to observe all students wherever they may be during the instructional activity in that portion of the room. Also, be sure that needed materials are readily accessible.

b.   Now pretend you are a student in the class. Enter the room, go to several desks, check for visibility, for ease of movement to other parts of the room, and for possible distractions. Alter the room arrangement if you detect problems.

CHAPTER TWO
CHOOSING RULES
AND PROCEDURES

Good classroom management is based on students understanding what behaviors are expected of them. A carefully planned system of rules and procedures make it easier for you to communicate your expectations to students. It also helps ensure that the procedures you set up will be workable and appropriate. The goal of this chapter is to help you identify a good system of rules and procedures for your classes.

PRELIMINARY CONSIDERATIONS

Rules and procedures vary in different classrooms, but all effectively managed classrooms have them. It is just not possible for a teacher to conduct instruction or for students to work productively if they have no guidelines as to how to behave or when to move about the room, or if they frequently interrupt the teacher and one another. Furthermore, inefficient procedures and the absence of routines for common aspects of classroom life such as taking and reporting attendance, turning in materials, or checking work can waste large amounts of time and cause students' attention and interest to wane. A brief example of a classroom with major problems in the area of rules and procedures is presented below.

> When the tardy bell rang, only a few of Mr. Smith's third-period students took their seats. Two played catch with the erasers, while others congregated in small groups and chatted noisily. Mr. Smith had to shout over the din in order to be heard: "Get to your seats. I need to take roll." Some students moved to sit down, while others vied for places at back-row desks. After much prompting, most of the students were seated and Mr. Smith began taking roll. Loud talking continued, abating only momentarily after Mr. Smith called repeatedly for silence. After ten minutes roll call was finally completed. Mr. Smith then asked students to get out their books and homework assignment. Loud protests ensued as students insisted that no assignment had been given. Furthermore, many students did not have their textbooks with them. Rather than allow a large number of students in the hallways to retrieve their books from their lockers, Mr. Smith decided to conduct a recitation on the assigned lesson. However, by then three students had already left the classroom to retrieve the text from their lockers. Attempting to get the recitation underway, Mr. Smith called in vain for silence. He finally began to ask questions, but before he could select a student to respond, several others called out the answer. A chorus of comments greeted the responses. Mr. Smith tried to continue asking questions, but the noise from students' social talk made it difficult to hear. Soon paper airplanes began to drift through the air. . . .

Observers of this classroom might criticize Mr. Smith for allowing students to get away with so much misbehavior. "Be stricter," they might say. "Punish the misbehaving students." Or, "Develop more interesting lessons to capture student interest." Some might even suggest that Mr. Smith set up a reward system to encourage good behavior. While these suggestions could be helpful under some circumstances, they do not address the fundamental problem in this classroom: *The students have not learned the behaviors that are expected of them.* These students almost certainly know that many of their behaviors would not be allowed in other classrooms, but the problem is that Mr. Smith has not taught the students how to behave in *his* class. Areas in which this is evident in this example include (1) what to do upon entering the room, (2) behavior during roll call, (3) bringing materials for class, (4) completing assignments, (5) out-of-room policies, (6) talking during discussions, and (7) responding to questions.

Of course, just knowing what is appropriate does not mean that students will behave that way. (For that reason, this book will not end with the present chapter!) However, a clear set of expectations as to what constitutes appropriate behavior will be a major start toward the establishment of a well-managed classroom environment.

Finally, remember that the unique setting created by secondary school organization makes it essential that you establish a clear set of

rules and procedures for your classroom. You will need to work with five or more groups of twenty-five to thirty students every day. Generally you will be confined to a single room with limited space and materials; you will be responsible for teaching many cognitive skills to a diverse population of students; and at the same time, you will have to handle administrative tasks, arrange for appropriate materials and supplies, and evaluate students. In order to do these things well, you and your students need an orderly environment with minimal disruption and wasted time, leaving everyone free to concentrate on the critical tasks of learning. Carefully planned procedures help create this environment.

Definition of Terms

Rules and *procedures* each refer to stated expectations regarding behavior. A rule identifies general expectations or standards. For example, the rule "Respect other persons and their property" covers a large set of behaviors that should always be practiced. Frequently rules indicate behavior that is not acceptable, although teachers sometimes manage to write only those rules that are positively stated (for example, "You may talk when given permission"). In such instances the unacceptable behavior is implied (that is, "Don't talk without permission"). In addition to general rules, many teachers will have a rule or two governing a specific behavior they anticipate being an issue or that they want to prevent (for example, "Gum chewing is allowed" or "Gum chewing is not allowed").

Procedures also communicate expectations for behavior. They usually apply to a *specific* activity, and they are usually directed at accomplishing something rather than at prohibiting some behavior or defining a general standard. For example, you'll set up procedures with your students for collecting assignments, turning in late work, participating in class discussions, leaving the room to go to lockers or the bathroom, and so on. Some procedures (for example, safety procedures for a laboratory or for equipment use; student notebook requirements) may be sufficiently complex or critical that you should provide duplicate copies of guidelines for students to retain, or you may have students copy the procedures into their notebooks. However, many procedures are not written, either because they are very simple or because their specificity and frequency of use allow students to learn them rapidly.

Identifying School Rules and Procedures

In most schools teachers are expected to enforce school rules. It is to your advantage to do so. A set of rules applied consistently in all classes and areas of the building is easy for students to learn. The rules also acquire more legitimacy in the eyes of some students because the

©1968 by Bill Knowlton. Reprinted from *Classroom Chuckles* published by Scholastic Book Services, a Division of Scholastic, Inc., by permission of Bill Knowlton.

rules are *everyone's* rules. In addition to rules and procedures that regulate student behavior, all schools have certain administrative procedures which must be followed by every teacher (for example, keeping attendance records). You need to find out about your school's rules and procedures before the year begins so that you can also incorporate them into your own classroom procedures. You can find out about school rules for students and administrative procedures for teachers at a school orientation meeting or from a teacher's handbook, a building administrator, or another teacher. Pay careful attention to the following:

1.   Behaviors that are specifically forbidden (for example, running in the halls, possession of particular items) or required (for example, being in possession of a hall permit when out of the classroom during class time; bringing a note for absence).

2.   Consequences of rule violations. In particular, you need to note the responsibility you have for carrying out the consequences, such as reporting the student to the school office. If the school does not have a policy for dealing with certain rule violations, you will need to decide how to handle them yourself. Thus, if it is up to the teacher to deal with the issue of coming late to class, you need to be ready with a system.

3.   Administrative procedures that must be handled during class time. These procedures include beginning-of-year tasks, such as assigning textbooks to students, collecting fees, and checking class rosters. Fee collection may go on all year, so you'll need some system of record keeping and a safe place to keep the money until you can turn it in to the school office. Some administrative tasks will need to be conducted each class period. These include taking and recording class

attendance in your grade book, handling previously absent students, and filing an attendance report with the office. You will also need a procedure for tardy students and for allowing students to leave the room once the period begins (not that you'll encourage it). Frequently procedures in these areas will already be established for the school. If uniform procedures have not been adopted in some area, talking with some experienced teachers about their procedures should be helpful.

Planning Your Classroom Rules

Once you have information about school rules and procedures, you will be ready to begin planning for your own classroom. Guidelines for rules will be presented separately from procedures.

Many different rules are possible, but a set of five to eight rules should be sufficient to cover most important areas of behavior. Six general rules that encompass many classroom behaviors are listed below. These or similar rules are often found in well-managed classrooms, although we do not present them as a definitive list. You may decide to use other rules (for example, a rule prohibiting a specific behavior) or different wording. For some teachers these rules might be too general and these teachers might like to have more rules with greater specificity. After each rule are examples of behaviors related to the rule. When presenting general rules to students, it is important to discuss your specific expectations relevant to each rule. During the discussion of the rules and related behaviors, it is best to emphasize the positive "do" parts of the rules rather than just their negative counterparts. When you do the former, you help students learn how to behave appropriately. You *will* need to be explicit about behaviors that are not acceptable when such behaviors might occur frequently (for example, gum chewing, leaving one's seat, calling out). These may be incorporated into your set of rules or discussed when presenting procedures associated with specific activities. However, there is no need to recite a long list of forbidden behaviors during your initial discussion of rules.

The set of rules you choose will be used later in several ways. First, you will discuss these rules with your students on the first day or two of class. If you teach at the junior high level, you will also post the rules in the room and/or make certain that students have their own copies. A posted set of rules allows you to focus student attention on and create a strong expectation about behaviors that are very important to you. If you teach in a senior high school, posting rules is not mandatory, although it is definitely recommended for ninth-grade classes; these students will be less aware than older students of what behaviors are appropriate for the high school setting. At higher grade levels you can usually rely on just telling students your expectations. There is also some difference in how you should present the classroom rules to younger and older students, but this will be described in Chapter Five. Finally, you may refer to specific rules as needed to remind students of appropriate behavior during the year. It should be noted that your posted rules need not (and cannot) cover all aspects of behavior in detail. Procedures for specific activities and perhaps some ad hoc rules will be needed. For instance, you may wish to keep your policies regarding student work separate from rules about general conduct. Examples of some commonly used, basic rules are presented below.

Rule 1. Bring all needed materials to class.   This rule can be helpful because it emphasizes that students must be prepared for each class period. It is important for students to know exactly what they are expected to bring to class in order for this rule to be followed. Thus, students should know whether to bring a pen or pencil, paper, notebook, or folder; and if more than one textbook is used in the class, which textbook. If the materials vary (such as a notebook being required on one day but not another), then some system will be needed to signal this to students. If possible in such cases, the teacher should develop a routine such as having students bring certain materials on particular days of the week (for example, "Spellers" on Thursday) or having students copy into their notebooks on Monday a list of materials needed for each day that week.

Rule 2. Be in your seat and ready to work when the bell rings.   Included under this rule may be procedures such as: (a) pencils should be sharpened before the bell rings; (b) paper and pens should be out and ready for work (including heading); and (c) warm-ups or other opening activities are to be started as soon as possible after entering the room.

Rule 3. Respect and be polite to all people.   Included under this rule are listening carefully when the teacher or a student is speaking and behaving properly for a substitute teacher. Some "don'ts" include fighting, name calling, bothering, and so on.

Rule 4. Do not talk or leave your desk when someone else is talking.   This rule addresses two student behaviors that, if unregulated, can become sources of widespread misconduct. Rule 4 is actually a more specific but less inclusive variation of rule 3. Because it is clearly stated, the rule requires little interpretation for students to understand it.

Rule 5. Respect other people's property.   This rule may include guidelines such as: (a) keep the room clean and neat; (b) pick up litter; (c) return borrowed property; (d) do not write on the desks; and (e) do not use another person's things without permission.

Rule 6. Obey all school rules.   This is a useful rule to include because it reminds students that school rules apply in your classroom as well as out of it. It also suggests that you will monitor their behavior in the areas covered by the school rules. Finally, including it in your rules gives you an opportunity to discuss whatever school rules are pertinent to your classroom.

Student Participation in Rule Setting

Some teachers involve students in rule setting in order to promote student "ownership" of the rules and more student responsibility for their own behavior. Student involvement can take many forms, such as a discussion of reasons for having rules and clarifying the rationale for and the meaning of particular rules. For example, a discussion might begin with the teacher making an analogy between society's laws and classroom rules and asking students what purpose these laws serve. Depending upon the age level and sophistication of the students, typical responses might include ideas about protecting individuals and group rights, preventing violence or destructive behavior, and permitting normal activities to take place. After this initial discussion rules can be presented one at a time. The teacher may first clarify the rule by describing (or asking students to describe) the area of behavior it covers. Students can usually supply concrete examples, although they will tend to give negative instances (for example, "Respecting property means not marking up desks or not stealing"). Consequently, you should be prepared to state some positive examples. The discussion of individual rules should also include a rationale for those rules whose justification is not obvious.

Another way of involving students in rule setting is to allow them to share in the decision-making process for specific rules. This is sometimes done at a school level by having student representatives or student council members participate in the identification of school rules. However, shared decision making is not commonplace in secondary classrooms for several reasons. First, the domain in which student participation is acceptable is limited. *Schoolwide* rules must be accepted as they are. Also, policies which are essential to managing instruction cannot be left to student discretion. Finally, it must be remembered that secondary school teachers instruct five or more classes. If each class generates different rules, posting them may be a problem and remembering which rules are associated with which class may become cumbersome.

Some teachers limit student choice to particular activities or behaviors. For example, if gum chewing is not prohibited by a school rule, and if you do not find it objectionable, you can give your students the choice of whether or not to chew (gum). It would be a rare class that decided to prohibit it! Another area in which an option may be available concerns whether seatwork is to be done silently or whether quiet talking is acceptable. When students are given such choices, you must also make them aware of their responsibility for making the chosen procedure or rule work and remind them that they will lose the privilege if their behavior warrants it.

It is important to note that many effective managers do not provide for student choice in rule setting. Instead, they clearly present their rules and procedures to students and provide explanations of the need for such rules. These teachers strive to be reasonable and fair in their rules and procedures: Teachers who act autocratically invite challenges from adolescents. However, a teacher who is authoritative, who establishes reasonable rules and procedures, and who provides an understandable rationale for them and enforces them consistently will find the great majority of students willing to abide by them.

Planning Classroom Procedures

If you have never analyzed the specific behaviors required of students in a typical secondary school classroom, you are going to be surprised by the complexity and detail in the following sections. Don't hurry through them, even though some of the items may appear trivial. These bits and pieces will combine to form the mosaic of your management system. Four categories of procedures are described: general procedures needed each class period; procedures for teacher-led instruction and seatwork activities; procedures for student group work; and miscellaneous procedures. The greatest emphasis is on the first two areas, although the third is very important, should you plan to use such activities. A fifth area, on keeping students accountable for work, is presented in Chapter Three.

As you read the items below, you can note ideas for procedures on Checklist 2 on page 34.

GENERAL PROCEDURES

Beginning-of-Period Procedures

On five or more occasions every day, you will need to begin a class period. It is important to conduct this activity efficiently so that you will be able to begin the content activities quickly. The following four items cover the things most frequently involved in getting the period underway.

Attendance check.   Choose a place where your seating chart, absence slips, tardy slips, and grade book can be conveniently stored. Typically this will be in your desk or at a lectern or table at the front of the room. You should have an unobstructed view of all the students from this location. Keep a seating chart for each class period, and use this seating chart to check attendance. You may wish to call roll for the first few days of class until you get to know the students' names and then use a seating chart afterward. After you fill out the absence slip for the office, note the names of absent students in your grade book. An alternative strategy is to call roll each day from your grade book and note absent students as you call the roll.

Students absent the previous day.   As these students enter the room, they can leave their absence slips at the location where you check attendance. You can sign and return the absence slip while you are checking roll, immediately after, or during the first seatwork activity.

Tardy students.   Most schools have a policy in this area; if yours does, be sure to follow it consistently. Teachers who begin to allow deviation from tardiness policies, for example, letting students slip into the classroom if they are only a few seconds late, will soon find that the rate of student tardiness will increase and that their beginning-of-class procedures will break down. Tardiness to class can become a nagging management problem if you allow it. If there is no specific school policy, you will need to develop a procedure of your own. Some teachers assign detention before or after school each time students are tardy without a valid excuse. Other teachers give a warning for the first incident and then provide detention or some other penalty beginning with the second occurrence of tardiness. You should keep a record of tardy students just as you keep a record of absences. A simple system is to mark a "t" in the grade book each time a student is tardy, just as you might record an "a" for absence. Another system is to put a spiral tablet or a clipboard on a table or attach it somewhere near the door. When the tardy students enter the room, they sign in before taking their seats. This preserves a record of tardy students and allows you to continue your instruction without interruption. You can then check tardiness permits at a convenient time.

Behavior expected of all students.   Students should be told what they are expected to do at the beginning of the period while you are handling the administrative tasks. They should know that they are expected to be in the room (some teachers require that they also be seated at their desks) when the bell rings, or else they will be counted as tardy. Once the bell rings, socializing should stop. Good managers often handle the beginning-of-class activity in one of two ways. Students may be given a regular activity that they are expected to perform at the beginning of every period. Some teachers use a "warm-up", in which several problems, a question, or some very brief assignment is displayed on the chalkboard or on the overhead projector screen. The question or problems may review the preceding day's assignments. An alternative to a work assignment is for the teacher to display an outline of activities for the class period. Students are expected to copy this in their notebook or on an assignment sheet. Another way to begin class is to tell students to use the time to get out any needed materials (headings on papers if needed, homework papers, textbooks, project materials, and so on) and to remain seated with no talking until you finish your administrative matters. This will work only as long as you handle these matters quickly and do not leave students in "dead time" for very long.

Leaving the room.   Occasionally students will need to leave your room during the period; for example, to use the bathroom, get a drink of water, take medication, or go to the library, to the school office, or to another area of the building. Usually schools have policies for handling these matters, typically requiring the use of a hall pass signed by the teacher or by office personnel. Most effective managers discourage trips to the bathroom or water fountain except for emergencies. Unfortunately, liberal policies in this area frequently result in classroom (and school) management problems.

A second area that is sometimes troublesome concerns whether students are allowed to return to their lockers to retrieve materials during the class period. Frequently teachers do not allow this at all and require that the students sit in class without materials or look at another student's text. In such a case the student does not receive credit for work not brought to class. Other procedures that are sometimes used are to allow the student to return to the locker to obtain the necessary materials, but to impose a mild penalty or count him or her as tardy. Whatever policies you establish, the overriding consideration is to minimize the number of students who go out of the room for noninstructional purposes.

Use of Materials and Equipment

Your classroom will have a variety of materials and equipment. Identify those things that you expect students to use, and indicate how these items should be operated and under what conditions. This should be done as soon as students are expected to use the equipment. There may also be a number of items in the room that you do not want students to use or handle. Identify these to the students and explain your rationale for keeping these off-limits.

Equipment and materials for students.   These items include the pencil sharpener, student desks, tables, special equipment such as microscopes, globes, encyclopedias, dictionaries, and other room materials. You will need to establish procedures for the use of whatever items you have in your room. A common procedure for the pencil sharpener is to request that students sharpen pencils before the tardy bell rings and not during activities in which the teacher is presenting or instructing the whole class. If students need to sharpen their pencils during seatwork, only one student at a time is allowed at the pencil sharpener. A variation on this common procedure is to allow two students at the sharpener—one sharpening and one waiting. If students have access to storage cabinets, bookshelves, or equipment in different parts of the room, you need to identify how and when these different areas and materials may be used.

Teacher materials and equipment.   Included here are the teacher's desk, storage areas, filing cabinet, and closet, as well as your own personal possessions. You should make it clear to students that they are not to take things from your desk or use your supplies without permission. Older, more mature senior high students generally do not need to be told this procedure, unless, of course, you observe students taking liberties with your materials. However, you should state the expectation to younger students, especially to junior high classes. Of course, you can be pleasant about it when you explain it, and the rationale for the procedure is so obvious that you need not dwell upon it.

Ending the Period

Just as one needs procedures to begin a period, so too are routines helpful at its close. Two items are of general concern: getting students and the room ready for the end of the period, and dismissing class. If room equipment or materials were used during instructional activities, these will need to be returned to their storage spaces. Any cleanup of materials and equipment should be accomplished *before* the end-of-period bell. Finally, you may wish to remind students of particular items needed for the next day or for other upcoming activities. Consequently, you need to leave sufficient time at the end of the period for whatever cleanup and announcements are required. If students have been engaged in seatwork with their own materials, then only a short time (less than half a minute or so) may be needed to put materials away. You will have to judge how much time is needed and signal the students when to begin cleaning up. Sometimes students will stop work and get ready to go well in advance of the appropriate time. If you tell students that you will always let them know when they should begin to clean up or to put their materials away, they will be less likely to develop this habit. Be conscientious about giving students sufficient time before the bell rings. They have a limited amount of time to get to their next class, and it is not fair to them or to their next teacher to cause them to be tardy.

The second item of concern in ending the class is the signal for dismissal. Many teachers prefer to dismiss the students themselves rather than allow the end-of-period bell to be the students' signal. This allows the teacher to hold the students in their seats if the room is not yet properly cleaned up or if an announcement remains to be given. If you wish to use this procedure, you will need to tell the students that you—rather than the bell—will dismiss them, and that they should remain in their seats until you give a signal indicating that it is appropriate to leave. If you use this procedure, some students are sure to test it by leaving their seats when the bell rings. In such a case you must be prepared to call them back to their seats. You might then dismiss all the students except for those who left their seats early.

PROCEDURES DURING SEATWORK AND TEACHER-LED INSTRUCTION

Good procedures for these activities are especially important, because it is during these times that instruction and learning take place. Good procedures will prevent or reduce the interruptions or distractions that can slow down content development activities or interfere with student work.

Student Attention During Presentations

It is helpful to consider how students should behave when you are presenting information to the class or while you are conducting a discussion or recitation. Typically students are expected to listen attentively to the teacher and to other students. (In fact, teachers often translate this expectation into a general classroom rule.) Teachers also expect that students should neither engage in social conversation with each other during such activities nor read unrelated materials or work on other assignments. The simplest way to enforce the latter requirement is to require that only books or other materials needed for the lesson be on the students' desks. You may also want students to take notes during your presentations. If so, you need to state explicitly that this is desired, and you will need to teach your students how to do it. Many students will be unable to abstract key points from your presentations, so you will need to help them by telling them what they should record in their notes, or by providing an outline on the chalkboard or overhead transparency. Also, if note taking is expected, students will need to keep notebooks, and you should show them how to organize their notebooks. This means presenting an example of a properly organized notebook and periodically inspecting student notebooks.

Student Participation

You will need to identify some procedure by which students can ask a question, contribute to discussion, or receive help without interrupting you or other students during whole-class activities. During presentations and discussions the simplest procedure is to require that students raise their hands and wait to be called on. In most circumstances it is not a good idea to allow students to "call out" comments or answers without raising their hands. Undesirable consequences of allowing call-outs include domination of participation by a few students, frequent inappropriate comments, and interruptions of discussions and presentations. Requiring that students raise their hands before commenting or asking questions gives all students an opportunity to participate. Two exceptions to the "no call-out" procedure are sometimes permitted. The first occurs when teachers want students to provide a "chorus response"; that is, a whole-class response to a question. This can be handled by telling students at the beginning of the activity that they do not need to raise their hands. Also, many teachers use a nonverbal signal for a chorus response—such as cupping one hand behind an ear—or a verbal signal—such as prefacing the question with a cue word such as, "Everyone, ..." A second exception may occur during activities in which hand raising might slow down or interfere with a class discussion. Again, students can be told that it is not necessary to raise hands during that particular activity.

It is worth noting that such variations from a standard procedure generally should not be used early in the school year. Instead, follow a simple routine for several weeks, until you are certain that students understand it. Then, if you choose to depart from the procedure, clearly communicate the difference to the students at the beginning of the activity.

Procedures for Seatwork

In many subject areas students are frequently given an assignment on which they must work in class. During such activities the teacher usually circulates around the room monitoring students and helping individuals. A number of procedural areas should be planned ahead of time so that you are able to direct student efforts while they engage in this activity.

Talk among students. Some effective managers do not allow any student talk during seatwork activities. They require that students work on their own, that they not seek help nor provide help to other students, and that they refrain from socializing. Other effective managers allow quiet talking among students when such talk is content related. You will have to decide what your policy will be. The "no talking" rule is easier to monitor, and you may want to start with this procedure during the first month or two of the school year and then try allowing students to help each other on a trial basis. If you decide to allow students to talk to one another or to work together during seatwork activities, you will need to establish specific limitations. For example, you might say that during certain activities quiet talking is allowed, but if it gets too loud, the privilege will be lost. Be specific about what you mean by "quiet talking"; that is, whispering or low-volume natural talking.

Obtaining help.   When students are working at their seats and need help, you should have them raise their hands. You may then go to them or have them come to you one at a time. This procedure will avoid the formation of long lines of chatty students at your desk. It will also allow you to control where you give individual assistance. If you choose to help students at a location other than their desks, choose one that allows you an unhindered view of the rest of the class.

Out-of-seat procedures.   To eliminate unnecessary wandering around the room during seatwork, you should indicate when students are allowed to leave their seats. For example, students may sharpen pencils, turn in papers, get supplies, and so forth, only when necessary. Trash may be kept at each student's desk and discarded at the end of the period.

When seatwork has been completed.   Sometimes one or several students will finish their seatwork before the end of the period or before the next scheduled activity. This circumstance is frequently handled either by having students complete an additional, enrichment assignment for extra credit, or by allowing such students to use the remaining time for free reading or to work on assignments from other classes. If you have enrichment activities that involve additional materials not in the students' possession, you will need to specify when these materials may be used, where they will be kept, and what the procedures are for returning the materials to their proper place. Note that if many students frequently complete their work early, this is evidence of insufficient assignments or of allowing too much time in seatwork activities.

PROCEDURES FOR STUDENT GROUP WORK

Sometimes an assignment or activity will require that students work together in groups. Examples include some laboratory assignments in science classes, the preparation of group reports or projects in social studies and English, homemaking labs, or study groups organized to accomplish specific learning objectives or to prepare for an exam. When small group work is taking place, the teacher usually monitors the whole class and responds to requests for help from groups. A number of procedures must be planned to help the small group activities proceed smoothly.

Use of Materials and Supplies

Frequently small group activities, particularly those which are run as part of a laboratory, will require the use of a variety of materials and equipment. To avoid traffic jams you must plan distribution stations carefully and use more than one, if necessary. When possible, save time by placing some or all necessary materials on students' desks or worktables before class starts. Be sure to check equipment for proper functioning ahead of time and have replacements on hand for use when needed. Student helpers may be assigned to distribute supplies and materials, to monitor supply stations, and to clean up work areas. If students need to bring special materials for group or project work, they should be told far enough in advance so that they may obtain them, and you may have to locate safe places for materials to be stored while work is in progress. If any of the equipment poses a potential hazard to students or may be easily damaged by careless use, you will need to identify safety routines and plan appropriate demonstrations to avoid accidents and damage.

Assignment of Students to Groups

This will be important for several reasons. First, students who do not work well together should probably not be placed in the same work group. Also, a group composed mainly of poorly motivated students is not likely to accomplish much. One strategy is to try to have at least two capable students assigned to each group and to spread the less-able or less-motivated students across all the groups. If each person's grade is then based partly upon the individual's accomplishments and partly upon the group's accomplishments, everyone in the group has a stake in what everyone else does, and the chances for a successful experience are increased. To obtain groups that are well balanced for ability, to discourage social talk during the assignment, and to save time in forming groups and getting started on the task, assignment of individual students to groups should be determined ahead of time by the teacher.

Student Goals and Participation

Students need to be told specifically what they are supposed to accomplish in their small group work and how to go about the task. It is a good idea to discuss with students ahead of time the different roles they might take in the group work. Preparing a list of steps that should be followed, and displaying it on a chalkboard, on an overhead projector transparency, or on a dittoed handout, can help the students monitor their own progress. You might even suggest time allotments for accomplishing each step.

Other areas of behavior such as out-of-seat movement, contacting the teacher, and so on, can be managed using the same procedures as have been identified for seatwork activities. Obviously, quiet talk must be permitted, but noise level is often a problem during group work. Impress students with the importance of keeping talk task-focused and quiet. During the activity monitor the groups carefully and stop inappropriate noise quickly at the individual or group level, before it spreads to the whole class.

MISCELLANEOUS PROCEDURES

A few other procedures merit mention. Although not all of these will be of concern to you, some may be helpful to consider.

Signals

A signal is some action, behavior, or physical prop that is used to obtain student attention or to indicate that some procedure or behavior is called for. If you always begin instruction by moving to a specific location in the room where you stand facing students, they will learn that you are giving them a signal that instruction is about to begin. Some teachers like to have a readily identifiable signal to notify students that seatwork or group work activity is about to end and that another activity will soon begin. Examples of such signals include turning the lights off momentarily, ringing a bell, or turning on the overhead projector. Any signals that you intend to use should be explained to the students. The class should not have to guess what you are trying to accomplish.

Public Address (PA) Announcements and Other Interruptions

It is important that you and your students be able to hear PA announcements. Therefore, you should explain that there is to be no talking during such times and that students should not attempt to ask you questions or leave their desks. Other interruptions such as visitors, office workers seeking information or forms, loud noises in the hall, and so forth, may be a frequent distraction in your school. You can reduce their effects by teaching your students a procedure to handle interruptions. A simple one is to indicate that whenever you are interrupted, students should either sit quietly with no talking if they have no assignment, read a book, or continue working if they already have an assignment.

Special Equipment and Materials

If you have special equipment or materials that are likely to capture students' immediate interest (for example a mini-computer or live animals), decide on policies for student access to these things and on procedures for their use. Let students know these policies and procedures right away. For most special equipment, learning centers, and special materials, however, wait until the first time equipment or materials are used to give a demonstration and instructions. You can also make a list of specific instructions and post it where the materials or equipment will be used.

Fire and Disaster Drills

Find out what procedures are used in your building. Because most secondary students know the basic procedures, a few timely sentences during the first week about the procedure for leaving the room (for example, by row) and where to go will be sufficient. You may want to post a map of where students are supposed to go. Eventually a schoolwide rehearsal will be held.

Split Lunch Period

Tell students whether they should clear their desks or leave their work out when they are dismissed for lunch. Tell them if it is safe to leave personal belongings in the room. Show or tell the class what route they should take from your room to the cafeteria and remind them of school areas that are off-limits and of proper hallway behavior.

CHECKLIST 2   Rules and Procedures

Area	What is Your Procedure in This Area?

I. General Procedures
  A. Beginning-of-period
    1. Attendance check
    2. Previously absent
       students
    3. Tardy students
    4. Expected student behavior
 	
  B. Out-of-room policies
 	
  C. Materials and equipment
    1. Pencil sharpener
    2. Other room equipment
    3. Student contact with
       teacher's desk, storage,
       other materials
 	
  D. Ending the period	

II. Seatwork and Instruction
Procedures
  A. Student attention
 	
  B. Student participation
 	
  C. Seatwork procedures
    1. Talk among students
    2. Obtaining held
    3. Out-of-seat
    4. When seatwork has been
      completed	

III. Student Group Work
 	
  A. Use of materials and supplies
 	
  B. Assignment of students to
    groups
 	
  C. Student participation and
    behavior	

IV. Miscellaneous
  A. Behavior during
    interruptions
 	
  B. Special equipment
 	
  C. Fire and disaster drills
 	
  D. Split lunch period	

SUGGESTED ACTIVITIES

1.   Identify the schoolwide rules and procedures you and your students are expected to observe. Be sure these are incorporated into your own classroom rules and procedures where appropriate.

2.   Read the case studies on the following pages. They illustrate classroom procedures and rules for most major areas, and they will be helpful as you develop your own system of management.

3.   Use Checklist 2 at the end of the chapter to help organize your planning of classroom procedures. Be sure you think through your expectations for student behavior in each of the general areas as well as in instructional areas that you will be using. Then develop a set of procedures that will communicate your expectations to your students.

4.   If you have trouble developing procedures in some area or are not sure that the ones you have selected will work, be sure to check them out with other, more experienced teachers. They will usually be more than happy to share some of their "tricks of the trade."

5.   Develop a list of five to eight general classroom rules. Be sure they emphasize areas of classroom behavior that are important to you and to the functioning of your classroom.

6.   After you have developed a set of rules, review them with an administrator or with another teacher in your subject area. If you do not know whom to choose, ask several teachers or a counselor for nominations.

CASE STUDY 2-1:
RULES AND PROCEDURES IN AN EIGHTH-GRADE CLASS

The classroom rules in Ms. Ashley's English class were simple: Be prompt, be prepared, be polite, and be quiet. When the tardy bell rang each day, students were expected to be in their seats copying the plan of the day from the overhead transparency. This plan usually included the topic, objectives, and materials for the day's lesson and the assignment for homework. Thus, their beginning class routine consisted of putting away their books, getting out their spiral notebooks, recording the date, and copying a daily plan. While the students did this, the teacher checked roll. If students were tardy to class, they immediately signed a tardy roster on a table by the door and took their seats. The penalty for unexcused tardiness was thirty minutes of detention after school. Students who had a valid excuse checked the "Please excuse" column on the tardy roster and left their "tardy excuse form" in a tray next to the roster.

The rule "Be prepared" required that students bring their materials and completed homework assignments to class each day. Students were not allowed to return to their lockers. Late papers were not accepted, but incomplete work was accepted for partial credit.

The rule "Be polite" required that students not interrupt the teacher or other students when they were speaking to the class. To avoid interruptions and to give everyone an opportunity to speak during whole-class discussions or instruction, students were required to raise their hands to get permission to speak. This rule also covered listening carefully when the teacher or another student was addressing the class. Students were not to use the pencil sharpener or do other distracting things during these times. Students were to treat other students with consideration.

Students in Ms. Ashley's class were expected to use quiet voices during activities in which talking was permitted. These included small group or class discussion activities or when the teacher had given special permission. Students were not allowed to talk among themselves during individual seatwork activities.

Ms. Ashley's students were allowed to leave their seats to turn in work or get supplies or materials from shelves without permission from the teacher, but if individuals wandered and bothered other students, they lost their privilege and had to raise their hands for permission. When students were working at their seats, the teacher often sat at a worktable from which she could easily watch students while she helped individuals or small groups. Students raised their hands for permission to go to the table. Sometimes the table was used for peer tutoring, which the teacher arranged.

Consequences for students breaking class rules or not following procedures were related to a schoolwide system of demerits. Demerits resulted in detention after school and in contacting parents. Ms. Ashley emphasized communication with parents about student behavior and work. She called students' parents with good news as well as bad, and each grading term she presented awards to two groups of students: those with very good attendance and behavior records and those who did outstanding work or improved their work during the term.

Each day Ms. Ashley used the last few minutes of class for cleanup and announcements. If students were working on seatwork, she had them stop, get their supplies ready to go, return materials to shelves, and check around their desks for papers and trash. Then she made announcements of upcoming events and reminded students of any unusual supplies they would need to bring the following day. After the bell rang she dismissed her students.

CASE STUDY 2-2:
PROCEDURES FOR SMALL GROUP WORK/LABORATORY
ACTIVITIES

The day before her science class had its first laboratory assignment, Ms. Davis discussed procedures and rules for group work and use of the laboratory facilities. The rules and procedures she discussed included the following guidelines.

1. Work with your assigned partner(s). Participate, do your share of the work, and be polite and considerate.
2. Raise your hand for assistance from the teacher. Don't call out.
3. All talk should be quiet and work related.
4. Stay at your group work stations unless it is necessary to get supplies. Don't wander or return to your desk until the teacher tells you to.
5. Read instructions on the board, overhead transparency, and worksheet, and listen to the teacher's instructions.
6. When you finish work, check over your worksheet to be sure it is complete and neat. If there is extra time, ask the teacher for more lab instructions. If there are none, read the references listed for the day's lesson.
7. The teacher dismisses the class. The class will not be dismissed until the laboratory area is clean.
8. Report broken equipment quietly and quickly to the teacher.
9. Obey laboratory safety rules: Never turn on gas jets unless instructed; never put anything in electrical outlets; never drink from laboratory faucets; stay out of the laboratory storeroom; keep your hands away from your mouth and eyes; wash your hands after laboratory activities; no horseplay.

Students in this class worked in pairs for most laboratory activities. Partner assignments were changed several times during the year, not at every lab session. On the day of a lab, the teacher began activities by quickly going over the objectives of the lesson, the grading criteria, and the procedures listed on the lab worksheet. If the laboratory activities consisted of several major parts, the teacher suggested time allotments for each part to help students pace themselves. The teacher also had a list of some references in the text and readings from other sources in the room for students to read for background when completing the worksheet, studying for a quiz, or as an enrichment activity in case a student completed all assigned work early. New words or terms used on the worksheet were defined. All this information was already listed on the blackboard or on an overhead transparency to save time. If the laboratory work involved many procedures, the teacher helped students divide up the work. For example, jobs for Partner A and for Partner B were listed separately either on the chalkboard or overhead. Two separate supply stations were often used to avoid congestion.

During lab activities the teacher circulated and answered questions of students who raised their hands. The teacher gave several reminders about time, providing a ten-minute, a five-minute, and a two-minute warning before cleanup. She allowed plenty of time for cleanup (usually at least five minutes before the end of the period). To make sure the class did not run overtime, she used a kitchen timer. Immediately after cleanup, the teacher had all students return to their desks. There she gave them a quick report on their behavior during the lab and also on any common procedural or academic problems. This information was helpful to students in future lab sessions and in filling out or correcting their worksheet for the day.

Sometimes this teacher used work groups for discussions, problem-solving sessions, or test review. For these activities the teacher decided on group assignments ahead of time and listed names of students in each group on an overhead transparency. On the transparency she would also indicate specific responsibilities within groups (for example, discussion leader, recorder, reporter, supplier). Tables and/or groups of desks were numbered before students arrived, and students were told to sit in the group indicated on the overhead transparency. In arranging seating beforehand, the teacher spread these groups as far apart as possible in the classroom. Then, as soon as class began, the teacher went over the objectives, procedures, and grading criteria for the activity before letting students begin work. To structure the groups' activities, the teacher provided a worksheet to guide students. As in laboratory activities, the teacher suggested time allotments, and she often used a kitchen timer to help her. Especially at the beginning of the year, the teacher reminded students of the classroom rules for group work. As students worked in groups, she carried a clipboard so that she could easily record participation grades. At the end of group discussion activities, students always filled out self-evaluations on how well their group had met the objectives of the lesson, on how well they had followed the small group activity rules, and on how well they, individually, had met their responsibilities to their group.

CHAPTER THREE
MANAGING STUDENT WORK

An outstanding characteristic of effective secondary school teachers is that they encourage student responsibility for completing assignments, using classroom procedures and practices aimed at keeping students accountable for their work. These accountability procedures help students develop good work habits, enable the teacher to keep track of student progress on assignments and other activities, and provide feedback and assistance to students. Because managing student work is such an important aspect of classroom management, this chapter is devoted to helping you plan an effective system.

In all academic core subjects such as math, English, social studies, and science, and in most elective courses, teachers give assignments that students are expected to finish, either during class time or as homework. Although long-term assignments are sometimes given, it is most typical for assignments to be due after a short time, such as at the end of the period or the next day. Students need to do these assignments in order to accomplish many of the teacher's learning objectives. If students are not held accountable for their work, many problems can occur. Consider the following example:

Toward the end of the first grading period, Ms. Peters noticed several disturbing signs of lack of student interest in completing written work in her social studies classes. The deadline had passed for students to turn in their first major project of the year, a report on their state's water resources, and fewer than half the students had met the deadline. Ms. Peters then extended the due date by one week. But even with the extension, one quarter of the reports were not turned in. Those reports that were completed were disappointing, because many consisted mainly of pictures of water scenes clipped from magazines and a short discussion taken from an encyclopedia reference that Ms. Peters had suggested as one resource—not as the sole source of information. Many of the reports looked as though they had been thrown together the night before they were due. With a sinking feeling Ms. Peters realized that if she graded these strictly, many students would do poorly. Because she had intended to use the report for a major portion of the grade, many students were in danger of failing. To make matters worse, numerous students had not been completing recent shorter assignments, and many of those that were completed were of poor quality. These had not been demanding assignments and they were well within most students' capabilities. The activities included completing worksheets and answering questions listed at the end of the text chapters. Ms. Peters typically had students do two or three of these assignments each week and place them in their notebooks. She collected them every three weeks and assigned a grade to the notebook. Of the students who did complete all assignments, quite a few did them poorly, with very sloppy or partially completed work. Again Ms. Peters felt herself caught in a dilemma. If she graded strictly (or just fairly), many students would fail, and she might face great resistance from both students and their parents. However, if she relaxed her grading standards, students would learn that they could get away with not doing their work.

It is safe to say that many students in Ms. Peters's classes do not feel accountable for completing work carefully or on time. The basis for the lack of student cooperation could be determined from answers to the following questions:

Do students know how each assignment contributes to their overall grade?

Are requirements for assignments clear with respect to standards for quality, amount of work, and due dates?

Is student progress being monitored frequently?

What kinds of feedback do students receive about their progress as well as about their completed work? How immediate is the feedback?

These questions suggest important areas of accountability. In each area Ms. Peters could have done several things to encourage students to complete assignments promptly and correctly. This chapter will focus on aspects of classroom procedures that communicate the importance of work assignments, enable students to understand what is expected of them, and help them make desired progress. The procedures that you need to plan concern your grading system, monitoring and feedback, and communicating assignments and work requirements. Each of these areas are discussed below. Checklist 3 is provided to help organize your planning in these areas. In addition, some case studies are provided at the end of the chapter.

YOUR GRADING SYSTEM

At the end of each grading period, you will need to record a report card grade for each student. How you determine this grade has important implications for classroom management. Grades are very important to most students (and to their parents), in part because they are tangible evidence of student accomplishment. It is therefore important that your grading system accurately reflect the quality of student work. In addition, you will want to use your grading system to help ensure that students complete their assignments by the due dates.

The first thing you should do before deciding on a grading system is to determine whether your department, school, or district have any policies that you must follow. Usually a school or district will have established a numerical standard for grades (for example, 90–100 = A, 80–89 = B, and so on). If so, you will need to become familiar with the policy and adapt your grading system to it.

After determining the relevant school policies, you should identify the components of your grading system. A useful principle to keep in mind is that the most accurate assessment of performance generally will be based on frequent evaluation of all aspects of student work, not just on what may be indicated by a few test scores or a major project grade. A system that assigns students a daily grade that contributes significantly to an overall grade allows for frequent evaluation and feedback and keeps students accountable for their everyday work; it is an important aid to

Reprinted by permission of King Features Syndicate.

the academic success of many students. In some subjects in which individual projects extending over several days or weeks are common (for example, industrial arts, home economics), a teacher can still examine student work daily and record a grade, or note "satisfactory" or "not satisfactory" progress. In addition to daily assignments, other frequently used components of grading systems are tests, papers, projects, workbooks, quizzes, performance, quality of participation (as in discussions), and extra-credit work. Many teachers include student notebook grades in their grading system. Students are required to keep all their work in a notebook, which is graded periodically for completeness and neatness. Often students must make corrections on all graded work before putting it in their notebooks. If you want students to keep notebooks, you should be explicit about what should be placed in the notebook and how it should be organized. In addition, the notebook should include a table of contents and/or a list of assignments. Also, a sample notebook can be displayed so that students can see what is required. While these practices encourage students to be organized and help them keep track of materials they need to study for exams, notebook checks are not substitutes for daily work grades. In planning your grading system, be sure that you can manage the bookkeeping aspects, and remember that you will have to evaluate twenty-five to thirty students in each class.

After you have identified the components of your grading system, decide what percentage of a student's grade each component will represent. Once you have established your system for grading, you might wish to prepare a handout for students explaining the basis for grading and describing the major components. You can have them take this home to be signed by a parent. This procedure has several virtues. For one thing, it makes very clear to the students what criteria will be used to determine the grade. It also informs the parents, who may then be of some assistance in helping their children stay involved in your class. Having sent this information to the parents, you may find it helpful later in the year to refer to it when discussing their child's progress in your class.

You will also need to set up your grading book so that important information can be entered into it. You will find it most convenient if you record all relevant information for each student in the grade book rather than keeping separate lists of student numbers and book numbers, absences, project grades, and so on. Leave an extra line between student names in order to provide extra space for the additional information. You can use the top line for each student to record a daily grade or homework score and to note absences or tardiness (write an "a" or "t" in the upper right-hand corner of the space, using pencil in case the absent student arrives late). Use the other spaces to record any other information (for example, quiz or project grades) that might be collected on the same day.

Some teachers like to use different color pens to highlight different components of their grading system. Using more than one line per student might require that you use a second page for a larger class, and thus you might run out of pages before the year is over. Get a second grading book if you need to. Finally, to enable you to turn quickly to the appropriate page, place small index clips (paper clips will do, if necessary) on the appropriate page for each class.

FEEDBACK AND MONITORING PROCEDURES

In conjunction with a system for recording and assigning grades, you should have other procedures for giving students feedback about their performance. Regular feedback is more desirable than sporadic feedback because it offers students more information and reduces the amount of time they practice making errors, if their performance is incorrect. If you give daily assignments, you will almost certainly wish to involve students in checking them, because your time will be too limited to check 125 to 150 assignments every day. Of course, you cannot expect students to check complex assignments calling for advanced levels of knowledge (for example, essay scoring). However, many daily assignments are of a more routine nature and can be checked by students. The following procedures will be helpful to keep in mind.

1.   Students can be allowed to check some of their own assignments. You can reduce the temptation to be dishonest by requiring that a different color pen (or pencil) be used for checking. When students do check and correct their own work, you need to monitor them closely and then collect and spot-check the papers yourself.

2.   You can also have students exchange papers for checking. Establish a routine for this to save time; have the papers passed in the same way each day. Vary the pattern every few weeks to avoid "too-friendly" grading.

3.   Describe to students how you want the checking done; for example, mark or circle incorrect answers, put "graded by" and their name in a specified place on the paper, put the number missed or correct or the grade at the top of the first page, and so on.

4.   You can record grades by having students call them out, or you can collect the papers and record the grades later. If students call out their grades, you should still collect the papers and examine them. Hold students responsible for accurate checking. If a student feels that his or her paper was marked incorrectly by another student, a simple system is to have the student write a note to that effect on a designated part of the paper. You can then verify the work when you examine the papers.

Another type of feedback includes having students keep their own record of daily grades, quizzes, and so on. Some teachers have students calculate a weekly or biweekly average from this record during a few minutes of class time. This type of self-monitoring keeps students informed about how they are progressing and makes obvious the effects of failure to turn in assignments.

When you have students working on long-term projects, it is important to help them make satisfactory progress. Break the assignment into smaller parts or checkpoints and then set deadlines and goals for each part. Check the work and give feedback at appropriate points. You might even assign a grade for satisfactory progress at major checkpoints. For example, for a long paper checkpoints might be established for (1) a description of the topic, (2) a list of sources and an outline, (3) a rough draft, and (4) the final paper. For a construction project a plan or description of the project or major stages in its completion should be evaluated.

Monitoring Student Work in Progress

Once you have made an assignment, you should give careful attention to student work. Sometimes a teacher begins work at his or her desk immediately or goes to help an individual student without checking to see if all students are able to do the required work. At such times several students frequently won't even start the assignment, and others may be-

"It's one of my better sales talks on reasons for completing homework on time!"

©1968 by Bill Knowlton. Reprinted from *Classroom Chuckles* published by Scholastic Book Services, a Division of Scholastic, Inc., by permission of Bill Knowlton.

gin it incorrectly. Two simple strategies will help avoid this situation. First, you can assure a smooth transition into seatwork by beginning it as a whole-class activity; that is, have everyone get out their papers, worksheets, or other materials, and then answer the first question or two or work the first few problems together as a group, just as you would conduct a recitation. For example, ask the first question, solicit an answer, discuss it, and have students record it on their papers. Not only will this procedure ensure that all students begin working, but immediate problems with the assignment can be solved. A second way to monitor student involvement in the assignment is to circulate around the room and check each student's progress periodically. This allows corrective feedback to be given when needed and helps keep students responsible for appropriate progress. Don't get into the habit of going only to students who raise their hands seeking assistance. If you do, you'll never note the progress of other students.

Long-Range Monitoring

Be sure to use your grade book records to monitor completion rates and performance levels on assignments. The *first* time a student fails to turn in an assignment, talk with him or her about it. If the student needs help, give help, but require that the work be done. If the student neglects two assignments consecutively or begins a pattern of skipping occasional assignments, call the parent(s) or sent a note home immediately. Be friendly and encouraging, but insist that the work be done. Don't delay making contacts with the home, and above all don't rely on using just the grade at the end of the grading period to communicate that a student's performance is below par. By then a pattern of poor performance may have developed, and both you and the student will find it difficult to recoup.

COMMUNICATING ASSIGNMENTS
AND WORK REQUIREMENTS

Student accountability will be greater when students have a clear idea of what their assignments are and what is expected of them. This means that the teacher must be able to explain all requirements and features of the assignments. However, that alone will not be enough: Not all students will listen carefully, some students may be absent when the assignment and requirements are discussed, and the assignment itself may be very complex. In addition, there is more to completing assignments than doing the work accurately—you must also consider standards for neatness, legibility, and form. While we do not want to encourage an overemphasis on form to the detriment of the content objectives, some standards in these areas need to be set. After all, good work habits, neatness, and careful attention to detail are valued attributes in most occupations. The following three areas should be considered.

Instructions for Assignments

In addition to an oral explanation of the assignment requirements, you should post the assignment and important instructions on a chalkboard in a place marked "Do not erase." Use the routine of requiring that students copy the assignment into a notebook or onto an assignment sheet. It is a good idea to record each day's assignment for a whole week (or more) somewhere in the classroom. This is helpful to students who have been absent.

The grading criteria and requirements for each assignment should be clear. Be sure you explain these to the students. If the instructions are complex, as for a long-term project, it is best to duplicate the instructions and requirements on ditto paper or have students copy the instructions into their notebooks. If in-class performance is to be evaluated, as in a home economics class or science lab, tell the students exactly what you'll be rating (for example, following correct laboratory procedures, working quietly and cooperatively, cleaning up) and how much weight (or how many points) each factor will carry. Be realistic in your grading criteria and systematic in following through with your evaluation.

Standards for Form, Neatness, and Due Dates

You'll need to decide whether students may use pencil or pen and what color or colors of ink are acceptable. Also, you need to decide and communicate to students what type of paper and notebook are to be used in class and whether students should write on the backs of pages. A policy for neatness should also be determined. Students need to know whether you will accept paper torn from a spiral notebook, how to treat errors (for example, draw a line through them, circle them, erase), and how stringent you are about legibility. You should also think about the consequences for students in this area if they do not do work properly. For example, will you deduct points or reduce the grade on the assignment?

Because some students may turn in incomplete work, you need to decide whether you will accept it and grade only what is done, subtracting the part not done from the grade, or if you will accept papers only when complete.

Decide on a heading for students to use on their papers. Post a sample heading and go over it with students the first time they are to use it. Remind them of this heading several times during the early weeks of school, and tell them the consequences of neglecting to use the proper heading (for example, five points deducted from grade).

Finally, due dates must be reasonable and clear; exceptions should not be made without good cause. Classwork should be turned in before students leave class. Accept late homework only with a written excuse from parents, or impose a penalty such as reduction in grade. The reason underlying this firmness is that many secondary students still require active help to avoid procrastination.

Procedures for Absent Students

A number of problems arise when students are absent from classes. They miss instruction, directions for assignments, and assistance they may need in getting work underway. Establishing routines for handling makeup work can be very helpful to these students. You will also avoid the problems that might arise if these students were to mill around your desk asking questions about missed assignments. They might also interrupt you to obtain directions for makeup work, or they might be unable to complete the work because they do not understand how to do it or what to do. The following items should be considered.

1.   As mentioned earlier, post weekly assignment lists on a bulletin board or keep a folder with lists of assignments in an accessible place so that absent students can determine what work they missed without interrupting you.

2.   Decide how much time is allowed for making up work, and stick to it.

3.   Set up a place where students can turn in makeup work and where they can pick it up after it has been checked (for example, baskets or trays labeled "Absent In" and "Absent Out"). The "Absent Out" basket will also provide a place where students can pick up any graded work that was distributed while they were absent.

4.   Establish a regular time, such as fifteen minutes before or after school, when you will be available to assist students with makeup work. Also, you can designate class helpers who will be available at particular times of the class period (usually during seatwork) to help students with makeup work.

CHECKLIST 3 Accountability Procedures

Area	Notes
I. Grading System A. Does your school have a policy in this area? B. What components will your grading system have? C. Weight or percent for each component? D. How will you organize your grade book?	
II. Feedback and Monitoring A. What checking procedures will you use? B. What records of their work will students keep? C. When and how will you monitor classwork? D. When and how will you monitor projects or longer assignments?	

III. Communicating Assignments
A. How will assignments be posted or otherwise conveyed?
 	
B. What grading criteria and other requirements will be described?
 	
C. What standards for form and neatness will you have?
    pencil, color of pen
    type of paper
    incomplete work
    late work
    heading
 	
D. What procedures will you establish for makeup work?
    assignment list
    time for completion
    where to turn in
    help for absentees	

SUGGESTED ACTIVITIES

1. Use Checklist 3 to organize your plan for managing student work. Note areas where you are not certain of your procedures and then seek advice. You should also read the case studies at the end of Chapter Three for additional ideas.

2. Reread the case study on page 42, used to introduce this chapter. Suggest some procedures or actions this teacher might have taken to prevent the problems she is facing.

CASE STUDY 3-1:
AN ACCOUNTABILITY SYSTEM IN AN ENGLISH CLASS

Ms. Clark posted a weekly chart listing daily activities and showing maximum number of points students could earn for each activity (a possible 100 points for daily work and tests per week). In addition, the students kept a dittoed copy of the weekly chart in their notebooks, recorded the points they earned beside each assignment, and had the sheet signed by their parents each week. Also on the chart was a list of books and materials to bring to class each day.

In addition to the weekly chart, the teacher listed daily activities in detail on the front chalkboard. Her lessons followed the order on the list, and several times during each class period she pointed out to students their progress on the list. When describing seatwork assignments, she told students exactly how much time they would have to complete each assignment; then she actively monitored students as they worked, circulating and providing assistance. During class discussions she made sure that all students participated by calling on nonvolunteers as well as volunteers at least once.

Students who had been absent were responsible for finding their assignments on the weekly list, conferring with the teacher before or after school, and filing makeup work in a special folder when completed. Students picked up papers that were handed back in their absence from an "Absent Basket." The first few times the teacher placed an absent student's paper into this basket, she reminded the class whose responsibility it was to get the paper.

Ms. Clark was consistent in her procedures for checking student work. She had students check their own work with red pen or pencil, or she had students trade papers to check. She always collected papers afterward. Sometimes she had students turn papers in for checking and grading. Students recorded their points on their weekly assignment sheets when the papers were handed back. All papers for the week were handed back by the end of class on Friday. Students were expected to record their grades on their assignment sheets and have their parents sign them by Tuesday of the next week.

CASE STUDY 3-2:
MANAGING STUDENT WORK IN A MATH CLASS

An important tool in Mr. Richard's accountability system was a notebook he required that his students maintain. On the first day of class, he introduced it by showing a sample notebook. In addition to daily assignments and tests, the notebook included a dittoed grade sheet which was sectioned for recording homework grades, test grades, pop quiz scores, and a notebook score. Students recorded their grades on this page each marking period, calculated an average, and compared their computations with the teacher's to verify their grades. Major tests were put in their notebooks after having been signed by parents. The notebook also had a section for the class notes which students regularly took during presentations. Mr. Richard collected and assigned a grade to student notebooks a week before the end of the grading period. The notebook grade was given a weight equal to a major test grade in determining the student's course grade. Although he did not collect the notebooks until late in the grading period, Mr. Richard always checked each student's notebook several times before collecting it. The first time he checked the notebooks, shortly after the beginning of the grading period, Mr. Richard simply looked for correct form and made sure that each student had begun using a notebook. Several weeks later he would check to be certain that the students were including the appropriate material and continuing to follow correct procedures.

Each day's assignment was written on the front board. Beginning on the fourth day of school, students did warm-up problems immediately upon entering the room. These problems were displayed on the overhead projector screen, and students were to hand in their work when the teacher finished checking roll. These daily exercises were always graded and returned to the students either at the end of the period or on the following day.

Homework was always checked and had to be turned in on time. Mr. Richard explained to the students that it would not be fair to those who completed their homework promptly for others to have more time or perhaps the opportunity to copy answers from another student's completed paper. When students were taught how to average their grades, Mr. Richard also demonstrated the effect a zero would have on their homework average.

When students returned to class with a homework assignment, they were given explicit instructions on how to exchange their papers and how to mark them. Mr. Richard told them to listen carefully to his instructions for exchanging papers, as he would have them do it differently on some days. One example was, "If I say, 'Pass it forward,' you pass it to the person in front of you. Then the student in the front of each row should walk quietly to the end of the row and give their paper to that student." When work was checked by students, Mr. Richard frequently asked who had missed a particular problem. If many students had difficulty, he explained the problem to them in detail. After the papers were checked, he told students how to determine the grade. Points were deducted if a student failed to use pencil or did not write out each problem. He then told students to pass the papers back to their owners.

Mr. Richard usually called on students for their grades and recorded them in his grade book. If students thought their papers had been graded incorrectly, they were to tell him the grade they were given and put the paper in a designated place on his desk so that he could check it at a later time. At least once a week, Mr. Richard collected students' papers and checked them himself. After recording grades during class, or when he returned papers to students, he reminded them to record their grades on their grade sheet in their notebook.

CASE STUDY 3-3:
MANAGING LONG-TERM ASSIGNMENTS

In Ms. Curry's science class students completed two research papers during the year. Ms. Curry had carefully planned the procedures to help students be successful on these assignments. For the first research paper, she assigned topics rather than allowing students to choose their own. An assigned topic made it easier for students to begin quickly and allowed the teacher to make some adjustments in the difficulty of the assignment for different ability levels of students. When she introduced the first research paper, Ms. Curry gave her students two handouts describing requirements. On one page was a description of the topic for the paper and some questions that it should cover. The other handout was the same for all students. This outlined general requirements for the research paper, a calendar of checkpoints and a due date for the assignment, and information about how the research paper would be graded. Ms. Curry went over all the directions and requirements with the students. One requirement was neatness. These standards were defined in detail and included information about acceptable color of ink, final appearance of the paper, the type of folder to be used for the report, and procedures for corrections. Another requirement concerned references and the bibliography. Students were to use at least three references and a standard form for compiling the bibliography. There was a specific requirement for the number of written or typed pages of text. The teacher provided examples of research papers from prior years for students to examine during class. She also indicated the days the class would be scheduled to work in the library. The checkpoints for the project included an initial approval of the list of references identified by each student. Ms. Curry also examined the students' notes. At both these checkpoints she gave students feedback about the appropriateness of their sources or work. Ms. Curry gave two grades, one based on the written report and the second based on the students' oral report to the class. Before the written report was due, students received a check-off sheet that they could use to determine whether they had met all the requirements before turning in their reports. Before the oral reports were given, Mr. Curry gave students copies of the checksheet she used for evaluating and recording grades for each presentation. She discussed with students each item on the evaluation checksheet.

CHAPTER FOUR
REWARDS AND PENALTIES

Although careful planning of class procedures and rules is a necessary part of good classroom management, it won't by itself ensure that you have a smoothly running class. No set of rules and procedures can be effective if students won't follow them! Whether students will consistently follow your classroom rules depends in part on the consequences—both negative and positive—of cooperating or not cooperating.

In this chapter two major types of consequences, rewards and penalties, will be described. A reward is something desirable that students receive in return for accomplishment, effort, or other appropriate behavior. A penalty is something undesirable that students must receive or do because of their inappropriate behavior. Only *planned* rewards and penalties will be discussed in this chapter. Some other consequences that occur intrinsically (for example, a feeling of satisfaction after completing a task) are not under the direct control of the teacher. Other consequences, such as reactions of other students or spontaneous interactions between teachers and students (for example, praise or criticism, smiles or frowns), will be discussed in Chapter Six along with other interactive skills and strategies for maintaining appropriate student behavior. Thus, it is important to remember that this chapter will not cover all the various reponses you might make to student behavior but will be limited to a consideration of planned rewards and penalties.

Some general guidelines should be followed while planning rewards and penalties. First, you should find out about district or school policies that might affect your choice of consequences. For example, your school system may prohibit the use of particular rewards or penalties, or the school budget may not be able to cover the transportation costs for a field trip promised as a reward. Likewise, districtwide busing of students or extracurricular activities may complicate the use of after-school detention as a penalty.

Your rewards and penalties should suit the behaviors they are intended to encourage or deter. Rewards too easily earned or too difficult to achieve lose their motivational effect, and penalties that are excessively harsh or too frequently used place the teacher in opposition to the students and invite criticism from parents. You also should be concerned about the use of reward or penalty systems requiring that you use too much class time for record keeping or other administrative tasks. Avoid using complex systems that distract you and your students from a focus on learning. Start with simple procedures and add to them if you are able. The suggestions in this chapter and the examples in the case study at the end of the chapter describe a number of possibilities.

Finally, your rewards need to be age appropriate and to have some variety. You can't count on a single type of reward to remain as a strong motivator for nine months. Instead, combine the ideas presented in this chapter with those of other teachers and your own experience to develop some alternate strategies for use at various times of the year.

REWARDS

Many different types of rewards, including symbols, recognition, activities, and materials, can be used with secondary students. Each of these types is described below with examples.

Grades and Other Symbols

The most prevalent form of this reward is the letter or numerical grade, although other symbols such as checks or stars are sometimes used with students in junior high classes. Good grades are a powerful incentive for most students when they are perceived to be a direct reflection of students' efforts, achievement, and competence. Therefore, it is important to tie as many facets of student work to grades as possible. In addition, you should make clear to students the basis for determining

Reprinted by permission of Tribune Company Syndicate, Inc.

grades, in order to help them know what they have to do to achieve them. Procedures for student· accountability have already been discussed at length in the preceding chapter, so we will not dwell upon them here.

One caveat is worth noting. Occasionally teachers react negatively to the grading system because they feel that too much emphasis is placed on grades and not enough on learning. This feeling may cause the teacher to project a casual attitude about grades and to be vague about the grading criteria. This is a mistake; the teacher is still required to assign grades, and the students are left with less control over their fate. A more constructive reaction would be for the teacher to work hard to make the grading criteria reflect the course's learning objectives.

Recognition

These rewards involve some means of giving attention to the student. Examples are the display of student work, awarding a certificate for achievement, improvement, or good behavior, and verbally citing student accomplishments. Some adolescents are embarrassed by being singled out for attention, so giving public recognition to several students at the same time is a better strategy. At a school or grade level, recognition rewards are often given at the end of the year or semester, with teachers nominating the awardees. If this is the case in your school, be sure to find out what awards are commonly given. Then tell your students what the awards are (for example, awards for attendance, achievement, improvement, honor students, hard work, conduct, good citizens, and so on) early in the year. Early discussion of these awards may motivate your students to work toward them. A similar procedure is to establish and display an honor roll (for example, an all-star list, honor society, gold record club) to reward students at the end of each grading term. Certificates, stickers with designs appealing to teenagers, or other treats

can be used in conjunction with the awards, especially for younger secondary students. It is a good idea to spread the honors around to include a good portion of your students. Thus, don't give awards only for outstanding achievement; have awards for improvement, excellent effort, good conduct, and so on.

Activities as Rewards

Permitting or arranging for students to do something special or enjoyable constitutes giving an activity reward. Examples are privileges such as free reading time, visits to the school library, or helping to decorate a bulletin board. A more elaborate activity reward is a field trip or party. Because school policy may affect your use of the latter activities, you should check these out before announcing them to your classes. You should, of course, be certain to describe clearly what students need to do to receive such privileges.

Material Incentives

These rewards include awarding objects of value to students. Examples include food, money, discarded classroom materials, games, toys, or books. In addition to ascertaining school policy, you will have to consider your own financial circumstances before deciding to use such rewards. Because you will have a large number of students and limited resources, your use of material rewards will be restricted at best.

When you consider what types of rewards to use in your classes, several factors should be kept in mind. Your rewards should be related to the student behaviors that are most important to you. Obviously, one such set of student behaviors is satisfactory completion of assignments, participation in academic activities, and attainment of learning objectives. For these student behaviors grades are effective and relevant rewards. Another set of important student behaviors are those related to following rules and major procedures. For these behaviors recognition and activity rewards can be used effectively. Some teachers hold competitions among their different class sections, rewarding the class that has the best behavior record, attendance record, or homework completion rate for a grading period. With the cooperation of other teachers and administrators, good student behavior can be rewarded by a party or dance at the end of the semester for all students who have stayed off the detention list and maintained good attendance records. An incentive on such a

grand scale requires much planning and effort as well as the cooperation of large numbers of people.

PENALTIES

The rewards described in the previous section will help motivate appropriate behavior, but they will not be sufficient to prevent all disruptions or other inappropriate behaviors. Penalties are necessary to deter violations of rules and procedures. It should be noted that penalties are not needed or even desirable for all rule and procedure violations. Many such violations can be handled by simple, direct teacher actions; these strategies will be described in detail in Chapter Six. However, you need to have a penalty available in case chronic misbehavior or serious infractions occur. Not only will penalties serve as a deterrent, but planning ahead for penalties will give you a standard, consistent response to particular classes of misbehaviors.

Students should be informed of your penalties and what they will be used for. This can be done when you discuss your rules and procedures. Of course, you should avoid a threatening tone. The best approach is to describe penalties in a matter-of-fact way and tie each to the behavior it is intended to deter. You do not have to describe school-prescribed consequences (for example, in-school suspension for fighting) or consequences for behaviors that are rare or for which the consequence is obvious. Such events can be handled when and if they occur, as long as *you* know what the penalties are.

The types of inappropriate behavior for which teachers often assess penalties include incomplete, missing, or poorly done assignments; tardiness; abusive name calling or other forms of aggression; damage to property; and repeated violations of classroom rules or procedures. Commonly used penalties include the following.

A Reduction in Score or Grade

This is the most common type of penalty for late, incomplete, or missing assignments and for poorly done work. When you determine your grading criteria, you should decide on appropriate penalties. Teachers often use the following: a score of zero or a grade of "F" for missing assignments (without a valid excuse), and a reduction in grade for incomplete work. Some teachers accept unexcused late work for certain assignments but reduce the grade; other teachers refuse to accept it and require that students turn in whatever they have done when it is due, accepting the consequences if it is incomplete.

Loss of Privileges

This is an effective penalty because it can be made to fit the "crime." For example, if talking becomes excessive during seatwork, the class can lose the privilege of talking (assuming that you allowed it in the first place). Students who abuse equipment or materials can be denied access to them for a period of time. A student who bothers others must sit apart from them. In other words, when a privilege is abused, it is withdrawn.

Fines

This does not refer to money but rather to "payment" in the form of (usually) repetitious work. For example, a student might be required to copy sentences, spelling words, division tables, or the capitals of the fifty states. This type of penalty is generally used for repeated violations of some classroom rule or procedure rather than for serious violations such as aggression toward another student.

Check or Demerit Systems

These are used in conjunction with other penalties. A student who violates an important rule receives a check or demerit. The teacher records this either on a chalkboard, in the grade book, or on another record sheet. Checks or demerits can be used on a daily basis or cumulatively. When used on a daily basis, the first demerit can serve as a warning; the second and any other demerit received that period causes a penalty (for example, a fine or detention after school) to be assessed. The slate is then wiped clean each period. In other systems demerits are accumulated, and the student does not have a clean slate each day. Instead, penalties are assessed whenever a predetermined number of checks or demerits has been accumulated during some period of time, such as two or three weeks. Frequently with such systems, if a student goes for a period of time (for example, two or three weeks) with no new demerits, the old ones no longer count against the student's record. Such systems require more record keeping, and they delay the administration of the penalty. However, for most students a warning is sufficient; little else needs to be done, because the students are able to monitor their own accumulation of demerits. The records also can be useful when chronic problems occur and a conference is needed to deal with the problem.

Detention after School

This penalty requires that students stay with you in your classroom or else go to a designated room monitored by some other adult. The penalty is frequently assessed for tardiness, unexcused absence, or violations of some major school or classroom rule.

In-School Suspension

This penalty is generally assessed for major infractions (for example, fighting, chronic tardiness). Students serve detention time during classes in a designated room monitored by an adult. Because the student misses classes, this penalty is used only for major infractions. Students are required to make up work they miss. In fact, they are usually expected to spend their suspension time doing the work.

Referral to an Assistant Principal, Dean of Students or Other Administrator

As in the case of in-school suspension, this penalty is best reserved for serious or chronic infractions. Follow building or district procedures and guidelines.

Restitution

This penalty requires that the student repair damage or pay money for replacement of lost or damaged property.

Confiscation

This means losing possession of objects forbidden on school property or in the classroom. Depending on the object, the student may have it back at the end of the period, may be required to retrieve it from the school office, or may lose possession of it.

"Back again, Master Biggs?"

In many cases the choice of penalties and their target behaviors are stipulated by school policy. You can determine what penalties to use in your classes by examining your rules and procedures, becoming familiar with any schoolwide system in use, and discussing possible consequences with teachers and administrators in your building. The following guidelines are offered.

1.   Use reductions in grade or score for assignment- or work-related behaviors such as missing or incomplete work. Other penalties, such as detention or fines, are usually not needed. When a problem of missing work becomes chronic, contact the student's parents, talk with the student, and try to get at the source of the problem.

2.   Use a fine or demerit system to handle repeated violations of rules and procedures, particularly those involving willful refusal to comply with reasonable requests. Such behaviors might include continued talk during whole-class instruction, or leaving one's seat. You will not need penalties to handle occasional occurrences of these types of inappropriate behaviors (see Chapter Six); however, students who persist in such behavior need a penalty for a deterrent. Give them one warning, and if the behavior persists, assess a fine or demerit.

3.   If you have a student who frequently receives penalties, try to set a more positive tone. Help the student formulate a plan to stop the inappropriate behavior, and be sure he or she understands what is and is not acceptable behavior.

4.   Limit the use of penalties such as fines or checks to easily observable behaviors that represent major or chronic infractions of rules and procedures. The reason for this limitation is that penalty systems work only when they are used consistently. In order for this to take place, you must be able to detect the misbehavior when it occurs. If you cannot, you will find yourself constantly trying to catch students who misbehave. For example, don't try to "fine" each student who whispers during seatwork. You can handle such events in simpler ways, and you certainly don't want to spend all your time checking for whispering behavior. However, you could use a fine if the student does not stop when you request it.

5.   Keep your classroom atmosphere positive and supportive. Penalties should serve mainly as deterrents and should be used sparingly. Try to rely on rewards and personal encouragement to maintain good behavior.

SUGGESTED ACTIVITIES

1.   Read the case study at the end of this chapter and consider how you might adapt the examples of reward systems to your own classroom.

2.   Find out about school policies that affect your use of rewards and penalties. Also, note any schoolwide system that you will need to incorporate into your own classroom's procedures.

3.   Review checklists 2 and 3 and identify the rewards and penalties you intend to use with your major conduct and accountability procedures. By planning ahead you will be better able to explain these consequences to your students and to be consistent in their use.

CASE STUDY 4-1:
EXAMPLES OF INCENTIVES AND REWARDS

Some additional examples of incentives and rewards that we have observed in secondary school classrooms are described below. These examples are grouped according to type, although it should be noted that some incentives combine features of several types.

Awards and Other Recognition

An attractive award certificate was designed by a teacher and used for individual students at different times during the year. The certificates were especially impressive because each was signed by the principal as well as the teacher. Students were recognized for outstanding effort, improvement, or accomplishment. To save time the teacher made many copies of the blank certificates before school began and asked the principal to sign them all at once. She filled them in as needed with students' names and accomplishments. The certificates were awarded both publicly and privately, according to the student and the accomplishment. (Note: Blank achievement/appreciation certificates can also be purchased from school supply stores.)

Honor roll systems are commonly used at the secondary level. For example, at the end of each grading term, a teacher having a low-ability class honored students who had improved their grades or performance by posting an honor roll he called "Best in the West." Students on the list received stickers, which they enjoyed saving to display on their notebooks or textbook covers.

Competitions

For some subjects long-range incentives are available in the form of city, regional, or statewide competitions (for example, spelling or composition contests, science and math fairs). Other competitions can be conducted within a school, with classes competing against each other, or they may even be limited to the classes taught by one teacher. The teacher can establish a reward for the first class completing a project or for the class in which all students complete the project first. Within-class rewards can also be offered. One teacher posted spelling grades by class on a bulletin board display. The class with the highest overall score at the end of each month received a special prize or treat.

Encouraging Improvement

Some teachers allow students to redo incorrectly done assignments to improve their grade. Students might be allowed to earn enough points to bring their grade up to a B level, for example. One teacher kept a chart on which stars were placed representing students' grades on assignments. For example, a gold star stood for an A, a silver star for a B, and so on. No star meant that the assignment had not been turned in. If a student redid an assignment and brought up its grade, the teacher placed a different color star on top of the previous star. Displaying the chart on a bulletin board also encouraged students to do their best and to avoid missing assignments.

Extra-Credit Assignments

Extra-credit activities are frequently popular with students, and the extra credit earned toward improving a grade is an important incentive for most students. One teacher kept an extra-credit logic problem on the side board, changing it every week or two depending on its difficulty. She also had extra-credit puzzles and worksheets on a front table. These puzzles covered material currently being studied by the class, and students were encouraged to work on these after they had finished their required work. They could also copy them and work on them at home. This teacher had students keep their completed extra-credit problems in a special section of their notebooks, where they were checked when the teacher graded the notebooks. Each correct problem was worth one point and was added to the notebook grade at the end of the grading period.

A science teacher kept a list of extra-credit projects for students to work on individually or in groups. Along with the list of projects was a description of the requirements for each project, its complexity, a deadline for completion, and the number of points earned toward a report card grade. English and social studies teachers frequently have book lists from which students may choose extra-credit reading. A form for students to use when reporting on the book should also be available.

Sometimes bulletin boards are used to display extra-credit work. One math teacher had a picture of a mountain, with math problems relevant to current lessons at each of several elevations. Beneath the mountain were lines for ten student names. The first ten students (from all classes) correctly completing the problems had their names posted under the mountain. When the tenth name was posted, the teacher taped a piece of gum or candy beside each name for the student to remove.

Special Activities and Privileges

Allowing students special privileges or permitting them to participate in desired activities is a commonly used reward, and it is often combined with another kind of reward such as recognition. For example, one teacher chose outstanding students each week, based on their attitude, grades, and attendance. The teacher would put students' names on a bulletin board display, and students would receive a special treat on Friday. The teacher also included in the special activity or treat all students who had not received demerits for misbehavior during that week. Another teacher recognized consistent performance by naming all students who had turned in all their work during the previous week as a "Student of the Week" and by placing their names on a special bulletin board display. After being named "Student of the Week" five times during a six-week grading period, the student was entitled to claim an A for one of the four major components of the report card grade. One teacher allowed fifteen or twenty minutes of free reading or game time on Friday when a class had been well behaved throughout the week. Another teacher made an "Activity Chain" from construction paper, adding a link when class behavior was good each day. When the chain reached a certain length, the class was permitted to have part of a period for a special activity such as free reading or a class competition.

Weekly Point System

Point systems are useful because in addition to giving students clearly specified incentives, they encourage students to take responsibility for keeping track of their own work. One teacher gave a dittoed handout to students at the beginning of each week, with the week's assignments on it. The students recorded points they earned for each assignment, with up to 100 points awarded weekly. Some bonus points were also available for extra-credit assignments, and the teacher could add extra points for good behavior and class participation. These weekly records of points were then used along with test scores to determine report card grades.

CHAPTER FIVE
GETTING OFF
TO A GOOD START

The first few weeks of school are especially important for classroom management because it is during this time that your students will learn behaviors and procedures needed throughout the year. Your major goal for the beginning of the year is to obtain student cooperation in two key areas: following your rules and procedures and successfully completing all work assignments. Attaining this goal will establish a classroom climate that supports learning, and it will help your students acquire good work habits and attitudes toward your subject.

Getting off to a good start requires careful attention to how you will teach your rules and procedures to your classes, introduce your course to the students, plan lessons and assignments, and decide on the sequence and amounts of time for various activities. This chapter will address these topics and consider some special problems encountered during the first week or so of classes. In addition, three case studies of beginning-of-year activities in secondary school classrooms are presented along with a checklist that will help organize your planning for the first weeks of school.

PERSPECTIVES ON THE BEGINNING OF THE YEAR

Several principles described below should guide your planning for the beginning-of-year classroom activities.

1. Resolve student uncertainties. When your students arrive on the first day, they will not be sure of your expectations for behavior or of your course requirements. Although previous experiences in other teachers' classrooms will have given them general expectations about what constitute acceptable or unacceptable behaviors in school, they will not know what *you* expect in *your* classroom. For example, should they raise their hands if they want to comment or ask a question? May they leave their seats without permission? May they speak to each other during seatwork or at other times? Moreover, the students do not know how consistently you will enforce your procedures and rules or what the consequences will be if they do not follow them. In addition, they will be unfamiliar with your systems for grading and other accountability procedures. Because of these uncertainties, you will be in a very good position at the beginning of the year to help students learn appropriate behavior by providing a specific, concrete description of expectations for behavior,

© **Leo Cullum.**

course requirements, and standards for work. However, if you do not take advantage of this opportunity, students may begin to behave in ways that interfere with good instruction and learning. You will then face the more difficult task of eliminating unacceptable behavior and substituting more appropriate behavior in its place.

Take the necessary time during the first few days of classes to carefully describe your expectations for behavior and work. Don't be in such a hurry to get started on content activities that you neglect to teach good behavior. Rather, combine learning about procedures, rules, and course requirements with your initial content activities in order to build the foundation for the whole year's program.

2. Help students be successful by planning uncomplicated lessons.   Your content activities and assignments during the first week should be selected and designed to ensure maximum success by students; students should feel secure and optimistic about their ability to do well in your class.

3. Keep a whole-class focus.   When planning activities for the first week, you should maintain a whole-class focus. Presentations and discussions should be made to all the students at the same time and not to parts of the class in small groups. Seatwork assignments should be the same for everyone, although you should have extra-credit, enrichment assignments available to challenge the students who complete seatwork assignments early. Restricting the type of activity will keep your classroom procedures simple and avoid activities that might make it difficult for you to monitor students or prevent inappropriate behavior. After your classes are running smoothly and students have learned correct behavior, you can use more complex activities, if these are appropriate.

4. Be available, visible, and in charge.   You must stay in charge of all the students all the time. Be where you can see what they are doing; don't get so involved working with one or a few students that you lose contact with the remainder of the class. Stay away from your desk unless absolutely necessary, and move around during seatwork to check on student progress. Doing these things will keep students more involved, and you will be available to assist students when needed.

PLANNING FOR A GOOD BEGINNING

Before you plan classroom activities for the first week, you need to have your room and materials ready and to have identified your rules, procedures, and consequences. If you have used the checklists and suggestions in Chapters One–Four, you are ready to consider a few final items.

Procedures for obtaining books and checking them out to students.   Be sure you know what procedures to use to obtain books, and have on hand any needed forms to record book numbers and names of students. If there is no special form, you can record book numbers in your grade book. Some teachers prefer not to enter student names into their grade book until sections have been leveled and enrollment stabilizes. If you choose to wait, you can record book numbers on the class roster sheet instead of the grade book and transfer them to the grade book later.

Procedures for checking out textbooks.   Be sure to wait until students have been assigned their lockers before you check out textbooks. Then have a supply of book covers on hand so that students may cover their books promptly. Many teachers check out textbooks by the second or third day of classes and do so during a content activity. A common procedure is to distribute the textbooks to students at the beginning of the activity, indicating whether the books need to be covered and any other relevant information, such as the cost of the book if lost. Later, after students have begun the seatwork portion of the lesson, they can be called to the teacher's desk one or two at a time so that the teacher can record their book numbers and note any damage to used books.

Required paper work.   Have all forms on hand. Use file folders for each class period to keep these materials separate and organized.

Class rosters.   Be sure you have these organized by period. Note any special students who have handicapping conditions that must be taken into account in seating or who require medication. You will probably be told whether you have any such students by a special education teacher or counselor. These professionals are also a useful source of suggestions for working with such students in your classes.

Seating assignments.   Plan to assign seats during the first week of classes. Assigned desks allow you to make a seating chart from which you can learn student names and also check attendance quickly. There is little point in assigning seats on the first day of classes unless you are quite sure that very few changes in your class rosters will occur. By the second or third day, however, class rolls may stabilize enough for permanent seating.

Some differences in seating assignment practices are observed in junior and senior high schools. It is more common at the junior high school level for teachers to assign seats, often alphabetically. At the senior high level some teachers assign seats, while other teachers allow students to choose their seats. In the latter case the chosen seat is the permanent one; that is, students are not allowed to move around at will. Also, teachers reserve the right to reassign students to different seats if necessary. Whatever the grade level, you can change seating arrangements later in the year to accommodate work groups, to move students who need close supervision to more accessible seats, or just to provide a change.

First-week bell schedule.   Find out how much time is available for each period during the first week. Some class periods may be shortened to accommodate extra-long advisory or homeroom periods. If so, find out which periods are affected and how much time will be available for each class.

Tardiness during the first days of classes.   Most teachers do not attempt to enforce their tardiness policies during the first two days of classes—students are still trying to find classrooms, and the time for passing between periods is not always predictable. By the third class day, however, it is usually reasonable to expect all students to arrive at your classroom on time. Tell them the day before that you will begin to count students tardy unless they are in your room before the bell begins to ring (or whatever your policy is). Then enforce the policy the next day and thereafter.

Administrative tasks.   If you have not already done so as part of Chapter Two activities, be sure you know what special administrative tasks are required during the first week. If you have a homeroom or advisory class, be sure to keep its forms and materials in separate file folders.

Rules.   You will discuss your expectations for behavior with your students on the first day you meet with them and as many times thereafter as needed. You can list rules on a large chart and post it on a bulletin board or a wall. You can also distribute dittoed copies of rules or display them on the chalkboard or overhead projector screen and have students copy them into their notebooks. If you have not yet decided on classroom rules, you should review the relevant section in Chapter Two. (If you are teaching upper-level senior high grades, providing copies of rules or posting them is optional: This is discussed later in this chapter under "Discussing Rules and Procedures").

Course requirements.   You will need to discuss course requirements with your students during the first week. You should outline the major requirements such as tests, pop quizzes, a notebook, projects, and homework, indicating how they contribute to the students' grades. You do not need to list each requirement in great detail, but you should indicate the major features. It is a good practice to provide students with a dittoed copy of your requirements—perhaps on the same sheet as your classroom rules. Some teachers have students take it home for parents to sign.

A beginning-of-class routine.   Decide what standard routine you will use to open each period. The routine should enable students to make the transition into your classroom in an orderly manner, ready for instruction. It also will allow you to check attendance and perform other administrative tasks quickly and without interruption. If you have not yet decided on a beginning-of-period routine, you should review the relevant section in Chapter Two. Whatever your opening routine, students should complete it without talking, remaining seated and quiet until you are ready to begin instruction.

Time fillers.   You should be prepared with constructive activities for occasions when extra minutes are available and students have nothing to do. This is especially likely to occur during the first week or two of classes, when the bell schedule may be altered unexpectedly. Examples of time fillers include worksheets, puzzles, and logic problems related to your subject. You may find books containing such fillers among the supplementary materials in your department's storeroom, in a book store, or in a teachers' supply store. You may also order them from teachers' supply catalogs. Further, you should check the teachers' edition of your textbook for ideas. Frequently a section of enrichment or supplemental exercises, questions, or problems can be used either as a seatwork assignment or as a whole-class recitation topic. You might also allow individuals who complete work early to have free reading time while they are waiting for the next activity to begin. You might keep a shelf of books and magazines for such times. Content-related materials are, of course, the most desirable items for such reading.

ACTIVITIES ON THE FIRST DAY OF CLASSES

For class periods of normal or nearly normal length, your first-day activities will generally include administrative tasks, introducing your course to students, communicating your course requirements and expectations for student conduct, and an initial content activity. For shortened class periods some of the discussion of course requirements can be postponed, and the content activity can be shortened or eliminated. First-day activities are described below in a commonly used sequence. Where significant variations in the activity or sequence may occur, they are noted in the discussion.

Before and at the bell.   Before the bell rings stand near the door or immediately outside the door. Help students find the correct room, and prevent groups of students from congregating nearby and blocking your doorway. Students will have an easier time finding your room if you post a sign with your name outside the door. Usually students enter quickly and quietly on the first day; however, should some students enter in an unacceptable manner, you can have them repeat their entrance properly or tell them that they are expected to enter quietly and without commotion in the future.

Greet students pleasantly, but don't start long conversations. Tell students that they may choose their seats for the day, and when most students have arrived, you should enter the room. When in the room, help students be seated, stay in prominent view, and monitor student behavior. When the bell rings, tell students your name and the course title (this information should also be listed on the chalkboard), and ask students to check their schedules to be sure they are in the correct room.

Administrative tasks.   Have all necessary materials close at hand so that you can begin quickly. You will first need to check attendance. When you do, have students raise their hands (rather than call out) when you call their names so that you can begin to associate names with faces. Pronunciations and preferred names can also be noted on the class roster at this time. If students must complete forms or class cards, or if you must take care of other administrative matters at this time, tell students what needs to be done and what behavior is expected of them; for example, "After you fill in the class cards, hold them at your seat until I call for them to be passed in." To facilitate the completion of class cards or other forms, write the needed information on the chalkboard or display it on the overhead projector.

Introductions.   Tell students your name and something about yourself, such as your interests, hobbies, family, or why you enjoy teaching your subject. If many students do not know each other, you can have students introduce themselves or you can use another get-acquainted activity. You can also have students complete a short questionnaire identifying interests, hobbies, or experiences related to your subject. Afterward, give students a short introduction to your course, including an overview of topics to be covered. Try to emphasize the course's importance, interest, challenge, and applications. Mention some activities that will be of interest to the students, so that they can begin the year looking forward to taking the course.

Discussion of class rules.   During this activity you will discuss your expectations for student conduct. Refer to the rules you have posted, displayed on the overhead projector, or made available on a handout. Read each rule and explain it, giving examples when needed. Describe the rationale for each rule and any penalties associated with breaking it. You can involve students in this discussion by asking them for examples or reasons for particular rules. Because students are often reserved in their class behavior on the first day or two of school, don't expect eager particpation in this discussion. If you intend to use a reward system such as an "honor roll," you could also introduce it now, or you might save this discussion for later in the week. If your rules do not already incorporate major procedures, you should discuss your expectations in these areas at this time. Students should understand what is acceptable with respect to student talk, how to contact the teacher for help, when movement about the room is permitted, and how to ask questions or volunteer an answer or comment. In addition, your procedures for tardy students and beginning the period should be explained. Don't go over procedures that will not be needed soon; you can discuss them when they are needed. Unless particular school rules are relevant for your classroom, you do not need to include these in your discussion; they probably will be discussed by a building administrator on the public address system or in a general assembly, or teachers may cover them during a homeroom or advisory period. Of course, if such a presentation has not occurred, you should go over the rules briefly during your first-period class for the benefit of students who are new to the building.

Some senior high teachers, particularly in the upper grades, prefer a less explicit approach to class rules. They do not identify expectations as "rules," nor do they post or otherwise provide copies of rules. They limit their discussions of expectations for conduct to a few major areas, such as tardiness and student talk. However, this does not mean that such teachers have *no* expectations in other areas of behavior—*they are quick to give feedback to students when the latter's behavior is not acceptable.* For example, if such a teacher is presenting material to the class, and students leave their seats, the teacher will use the incident to tell the class that students should remain in their seats during presentations. The advantage of this approach is that it invites cooperation by recognizing that many older senior high students are well acquainted with prevailing school norms and will behave acceptably with no prompting. The disadvantage of this approach is that it places a considerable burden on the teacher's ability to monitor students' behavior so that initial deviations from expectations can be detected. If they are not detected, students may believe that the behavior is acceptable; consequently, more inappropriate behavior may occur. Note that the less explicit approach to rules is the practice of only *some* senior high teachers. Other good managers at this level are more systematic in their presentation of expectations for student conduct. Finally, we note that the less-explicit approach should not be used at the junior high level or for ninth graders; these students benefit from the structure provided by an explicit set of rules and expectations for major procedures.

Presentation of course requirements.   Describe briefly the major course requirements and indicate how these will contribute to the course grade. It is not necessary to go into great detail about grading procedures or other course requirements unless some aspect of them will be used immediately. For example, you do not need to go over test or homework procedures at this time, but you should list on the board or display on the overhead projector screen those materials that students will need to bring to class each day. If you plan to give students a handout listing rules and major procedures, you can also include on it a list of materials and major course requirements.

When periods have been shortened, or in order to conserve time for a content activity, you may limit discussion of course requirements to the absolute essentials and wait until later in the week to fill out the picture.

An initial content activity.   Choose an activity that students can complete successfully with little or no assistance. This will leave you free to handle other matters and to monitor students. The activity should be an interesting one that will involve your students. Look in the teachers' edition of your textbook for ideas. Some possibilities include a review worksheet based on content from earlier grades, a subject-related puzzle, or a worksheet activity. You could also conduct a short demonstration or present an experiment, essay, story, description of an event, and so on, which you might then use as the basis for a short discussion. This could be followed by questions for which the students would write answers. Available time is a critical factor, so use an activity that can be continued the next day if the period ends before the activity. It is probably best to collect unfinished classwork at the end of the activity rather than to assign it as homework on the first day. You can then return it to students to be finished on the second day rather than relying on students to return it themselves—they may not yet have lockers, and some students will probably not have notebooks or other containers for papers on the first day.

Use the initial content activity for teaching important procedures. Begin the activity by stating what procedures students should follow. For example, if the activity is a presentation or a discussion, let students know what to do if they want to speak; for a seatwork assignment inform students how to contact you to get help.

When you introduce a procedure for the first time, follow these steps: Explain the procedure by telling the students exactly what they are expected to do. Use the overhead projector or chalkboard to list the steps in the procedure if it is complex, and demonstrate the procedure whenever possible. Then, the first time students are expected to use the procedure, watch them carefully and give corrective feedback about their performance. For example, you will probably have students use a specific heading on written assignments. To teach this procedure introduce it when the first assignment is given. Put a sample heading on the board, go over its parts, and then have students head their own papers. You could either check the students' headings at that time or wait until you circulate around the room after the seatwork assignment has been given.

Do not use small groups, projects, individualized instruction, or any other format that requires complicated procedures, extensive student movement, or materials that students may not have with them and that you cannot supply. Help your students learn whole-class and seatwork procedures before you try more complex activities.

Ending the period.   You should establish a routine for the end of the period that helps your students get ready to leave the room as they found it and in an orderly manner. Shortly before the dismissal bell (the amount of time depends on how much cleanup needs to be done), signal your students that it is time to clean around their desks and put their materials away. If you consistently give students ample warning, you can prevent their stopping work too early.

Some teachers prefer to dismiss the students themselves, so they tell students, "Please do not leave your seats when the bell rings because I may have an announcement to make, or I may need to give you materials before you leave the class. I will tell you when you can leave the room." Such a procedure allows the teacher to wrap up any unfinished business at the end of the period as well as to hold students until they have properly cleaned up the room. Some students will almost always challenge this procedure by getting out of their seats as soon as the bell rings, so be prepared to call them back and have them wait.

THE SECOND DAY OF CLASSES

If your first-day's class periods are very short, you may not be able to do much more than introduce yourself and your course and present rules and procedures. If so, you should begin the second day with a review of major class procedures and follow the first day's plan, beginning with a discussion of course requirements.

If your first-day's class periods are of normal or nearly normal length, the following outline of activities may be followed.

1.   Identify new students and get them seated. Have them fill out class cards or any other forms from the first day. If these forms are time consuming to complete, you can wait until the rest of the students are engaged in a seatwork activity before having the new students complete them.

2.   Beginning-of-class routine. Review your procedures for beginning class and have all students start the period with the routine. Perform your administrative chores, such as attendance check, at this time.

3.   Review your major rules and procedures. Provide new students with a copy of the rules and procedures.

4.   If you did not discuss course requirements on the first day, do so now. If students will keep a notebook or folder for your class, this is a good time to go over its organization and contents.

5.   A content activity. Many teachers distribute textbooks during the activity, conduct a lesson, and then give a seatwork assignment from the text. If for some reason students cannot be assigned textbooks at this time, you can still distribute the textbooks and collect them at the end of the period. Alternatives are to provide lesson materials, such as dittoed worksheets, or to give students a pretest or some assessment of readiness for the first unit of the course. This is an especially good idea if you have not previously taught the subject, the grade level, or students with backgrounds similar to those of students in your classes.

6.   Closing the period. Use the procedure you introduced the first day.

AFTER THE SECOND DAY

Continue using the procedures you introduced on the first two days, introducing new procedures as needed. Monitor student behavior carefully. Review your procedures and give students feedback when their behavior does not meet your expectations. By the third or fourth class day, you should be giving regular assignments to be done in class and at home. Check work promptly and begin using your grading procedures at once, so that students receive feedback about their work and are held accountable for it.

CHECKLIST 4 Preparation for the Beginning of School

Item	Check When Ready	Notes
1. Are your room and materials preparation complete? (See Chapter One)	_____	
2. Have you decided on your class procedures and rules and their associated consequences?	_____	
3. Are you familiar with the parts of the building to which you may send students (e.g., library, bathrooms, etc.) and do you know what procedures should be followed.	_____	
4. Have you decided what school policies and rules you will need to present to students?	_____	
5. Have you prepared a handout for students or a bulletin board display of rules, major class procedures and course requirements?	_____	
6. Do you know what bell schedule will be followed during the first week?	_____	
7. Is your lesson plan for the first few days of school ready for each class?	_____	
8. Do you have complete class rosters?	_____	
9. Do you have adequate numbers of textbooks, desks, and other class materials?	_____	
10. Have you decided on the procedures you will use for checking out textbooks to students?	_____	
11. Have you prepared time fillers to use if the period is extended?	_____	
12. Do you know if any of your students have some handicapping condition that should be accommodated in your room arrangement or instruction?	_____	

SUGGESTED ACTIVITIES

1.   Read the three case studies at the end of the chapter. They illustrate the beginning-of-year activities in three effective managers' classes. Use these cases to help plan your own lessons for the first few days of school.

2.   Use Checklist 4 to be sure you have planned all aspects of the beginning of the year.

CASE STUDY 5-1:
BEGINNING THE YEAR IN A
SEVENTH-GRADE MATH CLASS

FIRST-DAY ACTIVITIES

ACTIVITY	DESCRIPTION
Greeting Students	Before the bell Ms. Hunter stands just inside the doorway so that she can monitor the immediate hall area while maintaining frequent eye contact with students as they find seats and settle in her class. Ms. Hunter smiles and greets students pleasantly as they enter the room.
Introduction (2 minutes)	When the bell sounds, Ms. Hunter goes to the center front and starts class immediately by briefly giving some information about herself: where she grew up, how long she has been teaching, how many children she has. She also announces the course title and grade level and asks students to check their schedule cards to be sure they are in the correct room.
Administrative Tasks (10 minutes)	She calls roll, checking with individuals about correct pronunciation of their names. Then she passes $3'' \times 5''$ cards to the front of each row. Students take one and pass others back. She explains what to put on the card: phone number, address, birthdate, and class schedule. A sample card is displayed on an overhead transparency. While students work, Ms. Hunter monitors, answers questions, and distributes a list of supplies and a dittoed sheet of class rules and procedures.
Presentation of Rules and Course Requirements (25 minutes)	When students have finished with their cards, Ms. Hunter tells them to place the cards in the upper right-hand corner of their desks. She then begins to explain procedures and rules for this class. She shows and discusses a notebook they will be expected to keep, and she gives some information about how she will grade the notebooks. Then she discusses procedures and requirements that are listed on the sheet handed out earlier, explaining the rationale for various items and answering questions about them. Class rules are posted on a display near the door. Ms. Hunter reads them to the class and has students copy them down. She walks up and down the aisles, watching students as they write, and picking up the index cards.

84   Getting Off to a Good Start

CASE STUDY 5-1: (*CONT.*)

FIRST-DAY ACTIVITIES

ACTIVITY	DESCRIPTION
Content Activity (9 minutes)	The teacher assigns a math problem, written on a side chalkboard, for students to do in class. The assignment consists of a puzzle that requires computing several sums and differences that all the youngsters should be able to do. Ms. Hunter tells them that this assignment will be the first thing to go in their notebooks. Students start to work while she watches and circulates.
Closing and Dismissal (4 minutes)	The teacher tells students to stop work and get ready to leave. When she asks for a show of hands of students who have finished the problem, only seven raise their hands. She announces that the problem will be on the board on the following day also, and students will be able to finish then. She calls for the papers to be passed in from the back to the front of each row and then to be held there until she collects them. Students then put away their work. With about 2 minutes remaining in the period, all the papers have been collected, and students have their own materials ready to go. Then Ms. Hunter asks everyone to pay careful attention as she explains the beginning-of-class routine they will use tomorrow and every day in this class. She tells students that when they enter, they should immediately get out paper and pencil and copy and solve the review problems that are shown on the overhead screen. She will check roll while they work. The problems will be checked in class and turned in for a daily grade. She answers questions until the bell rings and then dismisses the class.

SECOND-DAY ACTIVITIES

Before the Bell	Ms. Hunter greets students as they enter the room and reminds them of the beginning-of-class routine she explained the day before.
Beginning-of-Period Routine and Warm-ups (5 minutes)	Students take seats and get to work on multiplication problems shown on the overhead screen. As soon as the bell rings, the teacher calls roll, talks briefly to a tardy student, and gives a new student a card to fill out.
Checking (4 minutes)	Students trade papers. The teacher leads them in checking their work, calling on different students to give the answers. Students pass graded warm-up papers to the front of the rows, where the teacher collects them for recording.
Administrative Tasks (3 minutes)	Ms. Hunter announces that she will assign seats in alphabetical order for the first term. Row by row, she calls students' names, and they move quietly to their new seats.
Presenting Procedures (12 minutes)	Ms. Hunter passes out dittoed grading sheets that she and the students will use in computing their grades every six weeks. Using an example on an overhead transparency, she goes over the grade-

CASE STUDY 5-1: (*CONT.*)

SECOND-DAY ACTIVITIES

ACTIVITY	DESCRIPTION
	averaging procedures to be used and demonstrates the importance of doing homework assignments.
Content Activity and Administrative Task (27 minutes)	Ms. Hunter distributes a worksheet for students to do in class while she checks out textbooks. The worksheet is a simple one which students can do without assistance after the teacher has demonstrated the first problem. The task includes adding numbers, determining whether the sum is even or odd, and shading areas of a diagram to produce a picture of the school emblem. Students work quietly on the assignment while the teacher calls them up one by one to check out a text. Students also cover their books. Some complete the puzzle from the first day of school.
Closing (3 minutes)	Three minutes before the bell, the teacher asks students to put their worksheets away. She briefly discusses the notebook they are supposed to have, showing the class some examples that students have already started. The bell rings and the teacher dismisses the class.

THIRD-DAY ACTIVITIES

Before the Bell	Ms. Hunter again greets students with a reminder of the beginning-of-class routine they are supposed to follow. The overhead projector is on as they enter. Students sharpen pencils and start to work. The teacher begins calling roll when the bell rings.
Beginning Routine and Administrative Task (8 minutes)	Ms. Hunter allows students 4 minutes to work on the warm-up problems; then she has them trade papers. She leads them in checking; then they pass the papers forward.
Content Activity (35 minutes)	Ms. Hunter tells students to get out their notebooks or paper to take notes. She presents a review of sets. Students answer her questions and write down the definitions and concepts she tells them to write.
Seatwork (10 minutes)	Students are given a seatwork assignment on sets. Ms. Hunter explains that normally this would be their homework, but since this is their first real assignment, they will be allowed to finish it in class tomorrow so that she can help and answer questions. Their homework for tonight is to finish putting together their notebooks. They will have a diagnostic test tomorrow. Students work on the sets assignment while Ms. Hunter monitors and answers questions. She also passes back the previous day's warm-up exercises.
Closing (2 minutes)	Two minutes before the bell, the teacher tells students to put up their work and clean up. She dismisses them at the bell.

CASE STUDY 5-2:
BEGINNING THE YEAR
IN A HIGH SCHOOL BIOLOGY CLASS

FIRST-DAY ACTIVITIES

ACTIVITY	DESCRIPTION
Greeting Students	As students enter the room before the bell rings, Ms. Holly greets students at the front of the room near the doorway, tells them to take a seat near the front of the room, and answers questions.
Introductions (1 minute)	When the bell rings, the teacher moves to the front of the room and introduces herself. She tells them how to check their schedule to make sure they're in the right room. She gives her name and its spelling, announces the room number and course number, and tells students the abbreviations to look for on their card. Then she pleasantly welcomes them to her class.
Roll Call (3 minutes)	Before the teacher begins to call roll, she explains to the students the procedures she wants them to use. She expects them to raise their hand when she calls their name and also to tell her the name they would like to be called. After roll call she records the names of two students not on her roll, after checking their class schedule cards.
Course Overview (6 minutes)	Ms. Holly begins by giving an introduction to the course. She displays an overhead transparency that lists seven major topics that will be covered during the semester. The teacher describes each of the items on the list and mentions several of the activities and goals relating to each topic. Students listen quietly and ask a few questions when the teacher invites them to.
Presentation of Classroom Behavior Policies and Rules (12 minutes)	The teacher distributes a mimeographed sheet summarizing procedures and requirements for the class. She tells the students to put their name, the date, and the period at the top, and to keep these sheets at the front of their class folders at all times. The information sheet contains three sections. The first outlines eight areas of classroom procedures and rules. The second describes the notebook that is a major requirement for the course, and the third describes the grading system that will be used in the course. The teacher discusses each of the items in the procedures section in turn, and the students listen and follow on their sheets. In this manner the teacher covers policies for being on time to class and consequences for tardiness, the importance of daily attendance, procedures for making up work after absences, turning in classwork on time and consequences for late work, keeping all paper in the science notebook and replacing lost papers, safety rules for laboratory activities, and routines for ending the class period and dismissal. The teacher displays the school handbook for students and tells them that they will go over the handbook in greater detail in class later during the week.

CASE STUDY 5-2: (*CONT.*)

FIRST-DAY ACTIVITIES

ACTIVITY	DESCRIPTION
Discussion of Grading and Notebook Requirements (10 minutes)	Ms. Holly then describes in some detail the system that she will use for determining grades in the class. One of the major requirements will be a notebook for all student work. She explains the requirements for this notebook: the type of folder, the importance of keeping papers in the proper order, the heading for papers, the table of contents, and the requirement that all papers in the notebook be completed and/or corrected before the notebook is turned in. After answering student questions about the notebook, the teacher describes the grading system that she will use. (Tests in the class count 40 percent of the grade. Daily work is also 40 percent, and the notebook is 20 percent. There will be two or three unit exams during each six-week period.) The teacher also mentions extra-credit projects which can be done later in the grading period.
Filling Out Information Cards, Checking Out Books, and Covering Books (12 minutes)	After this presentation of procedures and requirements for the course, Ms. Holly asks students to fill out information cards. She shows a model card on an overhead transparency and goes over the items with students. Then she explains to them the procedure they will use for checking out books and covering them. Because students have been assigned their lockers, the teacher passes out textbooks and directs students to check through them for damage and write their names on the front cover. The teacher has the name of the text and the information that students are supposed to write in their book displayed on the overhead transparency along with instructions for recording the number neatly on the class card, covering the book, and information about the cost of the book. The teacher passes out book covers, and students cover their books after completing their information cards.
Discussion of Textbook Reading Assignment (8 minutes)	Ms. Holly then asks students to look at a page in their text, and she introduces them to its format. She leads a discussion on how students can find the chapter objectives and use chapter titles and subtitles, along with the glossary and dictionary, to guide them in their reading. The teacher discusses their homework reading assignment (written on the chalkboard) briefly.
Seatwork (5 minutes)	Ms. Holly distributes dittoed assignment sheets and gives directions for answering questions on the sheets as part of the homework assignment. This assignment is a simple introduction to using different parts of the textbook to locate information. Students begin work on their reading assignment or on their ditto assignment while the teacher monitors and confers with one student about registration. When the bell rings signaling the end of class, the reacher reminds students of what to bring tomorrow and dismisses them.

CASE STUDY 5-2: (*CONT.*)

SECOND-DAY ACTIVITIES

ACTIVITY	DESCRIPTION
Seatwork, Roll Call, and Other Administrative Matters (6 minutes)	As soon as the tardy bell rings, Ms. Holly distributes a dittoed sheet for students to work on. This task is an extension of the students' classwork assignment from the previous day, an easy assignment in which students used the table of contents and book index to locate specific information. The purpose of this assignment is to acquaint students with the contents of their biology textbook. While students work on the ditto, the teacher calls roll and takes care of two new students.
Discussion of Homework and Seatwork Assignments (12 minutes)	The teacher calls for the students' attention and begins asking questions from the previously assigned worksheets. Students volunteer answers, and the teacher leads a discussion. Students check their own papers during this discussion.
Presentation and Discussion of Textbook Chapter (30 minutes)	Ms. Holly distributes a ditto consisting of an outline of the chapter which students were to have read for homework and about which the teacher now presents a lecture and questions students. The teacher also has a copy of the outline displayed on the overhead transparency. Students take notes on their outline as the teacher discusses the content.
End-of-Class Routine (2 minutes)	The teacher ends her discussion of the first chapter and explains requirements for a short homework assignment for the following day. She then reminds the students that each day they are to get ready to leave class by checking their work area for neatness and making sure they have all their belongings and materials ready. She shows them where the homework assignment will be written each day on the front chalkboard along with the list of what they will need to bring to class the next day. Students are told to be sure to check this every day. The teacher answers several questions from students and leads an informal discussion until the bell rings. She then dismisses the class.

CASE STUDY 5-3:
BEGINNING THE YEAR IN AN
EIGHTH-GRADE ENGLISH CLASS

FIRST-DAY ACTIVITIES

ACTIVITY	DESCRIPTION
Before the Bell	As students enter Mr. Franklin stands at the front of the room. He has arranged his materials and notes on a speaking podium there. He smiles at students, telling them to take seats quickly because he will begin class immediately at the bell.

CASE STUDY 5-3: (*CONT.*)

FIRST-DAY ACTIVITIES

ACTIVITY	DESCRIPTION
Administrative Tasks (5 minutes)	As soon as class begins, the teacher gets the students' attention and directs them to take out paper and pen while he checks attendance. He calls each student's name, checking on correct pronunciation and preferred nicknames.
Introductions (6 minutes)	He begins introductions by asking students to write his name, the course title, and the room number on the first line of their papers. The information is written on the front board. The teacher tells a little about himself and his background. He talks about the importance of the course (English) and mentions a few of the topics the class will cover.
Presentation of Rules and Procedures (15 minutes)	Mr. Franklin explains that today they will discuss rules and procedures for the class so that students will know just what he expects from them. He also tells them that they will be expected to take notes (with his help); they will finish the notes on rules and procedures tomorrow and then keep them in their class notebooks. He states the importance of neatness on this paper as on all papers they will be doing. In the ensuing discussion of basic rules and procedures, the teacher shows each requirement in a short sentence on the overhead screen, repeats it, and allows time for students to copy it from the screen. Besides presenting the rules, he describes materials students will need for class. He circulates around the room as he talks, maintaining eye contact with students.
Administrative Tasks (5 minutes)	As students put their notes away, Mr. Franklin distributes index cards. He puts a transparency on the overhead projector, showing the items of information he wants each student to list on the card.
Content Activity (22 minutes)	As students hand in the index cards, Mr. Franklin passes out a dittoed sheet for a short writing activity consisting of a number of incomplete sentences about the students themselves. Students are to complete these sentences with an opinion. After about 5 minutes, when all students have finished, Mr. Franklin tells the students to get out another piece of paper. Using a poster display he has prepared, he shows students how to head their papers and gives them a short assignment to be handed in today at the end of class. The task is to write a paragraph elaborating on one of the sentences from the dittoed inventory. The teacher explains that he wants to learn more about the students and identify some areas they will need to work on during writing instruction. Students work on this activity while the teacher monitors.
Closing and Dismissal (2 minutes)	Just before the bell rings, Mr. Franklin has students pass their papers forward and prepare to leave. They leave when dismissed by the teacher.

SECOND-DAY ACTIVITIES

Greeting Students	As students enter the room on the second day of school, Mr. Franklin reminds them of the class rule about being seated when the bell rings. They get seated.

CASE STUDY 5-3: (*CONT.*)

SECOND-DAY ACTIVITIES

ACTIVITY	DESCRIPTION
Administrative Tasks (5 minutes)	As soon as the bell rings, he announces that students should get out paper and pen. While they do this, he calls roll. A new student is asked to see the teacher after class to get a copy of the information presented yesterday.
Beginning Routine (12 minutes)	Mr. Franklin introduces a journal-writing activity that will be done at the beginning of each class period. He explains what information should be on the cover of the journal folder, what information should be on each day's entry, and other details such as when to get the folder, how long the activity will last, and how the journals will be graded. He then explains the topic for the day and tells students what to do if they run out of things to write. Students then write for 5 minutes. When the teacher tells them to stop, he describes to them how to place the papers in the folders and pass them in.
Presenting Procedures and Information (10 minutes)	The teacher reviews some basic rules and procedures which were presented and discussed on the first day of school. He then presents additional course requirements and information, reading each item aloud and discussing it. Students are given time to copy the procedures and requirements for their notebooks. Mr. Franklin discusses grading, the weekly work schedule for different English-class activities, notebook requirements, and the assignment board on which daily topics and supply requirements are listed in advance for each week. Students are told to keep this information at the front of their notebooks.
Testing (12 minutes)	Mr. Franklin then instructs students to head a piece of paper for a diagnostic grammar test. He reminds them of the correct heading form presented the first day and now displayed on a poster on a bulletin board. He watches while students prepare their papers. When they have finished, he explains the purpose of the test: determining what level of grammar work students are ready for.
Content Activity (13 minutes)	After the test has been completed, the teacher gives the class general feedback on the previous day's writing activity. He discusses areas in which students were skilled and areas in need of work. He also mentions some interesting things he read, without using any students' names.
Closing and Dismissal	The bell rings during this discussion, and the teacher asks students to check around their desks for belongings or trash. He then dismisses the class.

THIRD-DAY ACTIVITIES

Administrative Task (6 minutes)	Mr. Franklin seats students in alphabetical order while checking attendance. He has students prepare to do the journal-writing activity.
Beginning Routine (8 minutes)	Mr. Franklin reviews the procedures for the journal-writing activity and introduces the topic for today. While students are writing, he completes the roll and then circulates among the students. When

CASE STUDY 5-3: (*CONT.*)

THIRD-DAY ACTIVITIES

ACTIVITY	DESCRIPTION
	journal folders have been passed to the front of the row, he asks a student to be the helper, collecting folders each day. While the folders are being put away, Mr. Franklin asks students to take out a pen and the dictionaries that are already placed in their desks. He then passes out dittoed exercises.
Content Activity *and* Administrative Task (40 minutes)	Mr. Franklin introduces a content activity: completing a worksheet on word roots. He explains the objectives of the assignment and leads the students in doing several examples. After checking to be sure all students understand the assignment, he tells them that they have 30 minutes to complete it. The teacher also explains that the class will be completing an administrative task: checking out books. Each student will be called to the teacher's desk to pick up a grammar and a literature book and two covers. Students are to complete and turn in their assignment before covering books. The teacher also has a crossword puzzle on root words for early finishers. The teacher finishes checking out books before most students have finished their assignment. He gives an 8-minute warning to workers, then circulates and answers questions. Students cover books or work on puzzles when they have turned in their papers.
Closing and Dismissal (2 minutes)	When there are 2 minutes left in class, Mr. Franklin asks students to turn in all papers and prepare to leave. The bell rings, and the teacher dismisses the class.

CHAPTER SIX
MAINTAINING GOOD STUDENT BEHAVIOR

As you have seen in the first five chapters, good classroom management depends on very careful planning of classroom organization, rules, procedures, and initial activities. All the planning and preparation will pay large dividends once the students arrive, because you will be ready for them. However, being ready is not sufficient to sustain good behavior throughout the year. You will need to be actively involved in maintaining student cooperation and compliance with necessary classroom rules and procedures. You cannot assume that students will behave appropriately just because you once discussed what was expected of them.

In particular, don't be lulled into complacency by the good behavior of your students during the first few days of school. Most classes are quiet and subdued on the first day or two of school without careful attention being paid to maintaining good behavior; but a class that seemed to begin very well may ultimately become disruptive and difficult to control. The following brief example illustrates what can happen in such a class and suggests some of the reasons why management problems can develop.

Ms. Johnson carefully discussed her classroom rules and procedures each period on the first two days of class, and students were generally well behaved. However, by the beginning of the second week, problems have begun to occur. While making presentations to the class, Ms. Johnson stands at the front chalkboard in order to jot down important points. When she turns away from students to write on the board, students at the back of the room begin talking and passing notes. During seatwork assignments, if Ms. Johnson reprimands students for talking, they compain that they don't understand what to do and that they are just seeking help from each other. But when the teacher allows students to help each other during seatwork, by the end of the period, everyone is talking, few are working, and the noise level is very high.

During discussion students at first raised their hands to speak, as Ms. Johnson had requested, but some students occasionally called out answers and comments. Rather than ignore these responses, Ms. Johnson began to accept them when they were substantive. Now, as more and more students disregard the hand-raising procedure, class discussions and presentations are interrupted frequently, and some students become loud and attention seeking. Because discussion activities do not seem to work very well, Ms. Johnson has begun to reduce the amount of time spent on these activities and to assign more seatwork.

During seatwork activities Ms. Johnson often sits at her desk checking papers or helping students who come up to her desk. Most of the students work at the beginning of the activities, but when some students won't or can't do the work, they often become noisy and distracting to others. Then Ms. Johnson has a difficult time getting order restored and returning students to their work.

Problems such as those occurring in Ms. Johnson's class often have a gradual onset, developing over several weeks or even months. It is usually possible to avoid these problems, but doing so depends on understanding why the problems occur and what to do to prevent them. Because they develop gradually, the causes are not always apparent to the teacher or even to an observer unfamiliar with the history of the classroom. However, the capsule account of events in Ms. Johnson's class suggests several reasons why things are beginning to go awry. One problem is that Ms. Johnson is not monitoring student behavior carefully enough. Note passing, talking, and work avoidance are going undetected until the noise or commotion level is high. In addition, the teacher is not actively checking student progress on assignments. This reduces student accountability and prevents the teacher from providing the assistance that students may need to achieve the learning objectives.

A second problem is that Ms. Johnson is being inconsistent in her use of procedures and in her reaction to students when they do not follow the procedures. By accepting some call-outs and allowing noisy talk during seatwork, she invites students to continue to test the limits until the procedures finally break down.

A third problem, related to the first two, is that too many inappropriate behaviors are being ignored. As a result, minor events are escalating into major disruptions involving substantial numbers of students.

These problems can be prevented or dealt with by following three important guidelines:

Monitor student behavior carefully.
Be consistent in the use of procedures, rules, and consequences.
Deal with inappropriate behavior promptly.

The remainder of the chapter discusses how these guidelines can be implemented.

MONITORING STUDENT BEHAVIOR

To be an effective monitor of classroom behavior, you must know what t o look for. Two categories of behavior are especially important:

Student involvement in learning activities.
Student compliance with classroom rules and procedures.

Student involvement is indicated by many behaviors, including attention during presentations and discussions, and progress in seatwork and other assignments. Students' compliance with classroom rules and procedures will be easy to monitor if you have a clear set of expectations for student behavior and have communicated these to the class.

Monitoring student behavior during presentations requires that you stand or sit so that you can see the faces of all the students and that you scan the room frequently. Some teachers are not very good monitors of student behavior during whole-class activities because they focus their attention on a limited number of students (for example, those seated in

© **Reprinted by permission of Tribune Company Syndicate, Inc.**

the middle rows and at the front desks). Other teachers "talk to the chalkboard." In either case the teacher does not have a very clear perception of overall student response to the presentation or of what may be occurring at the periphery of the class. During your presentations, therefore, try to move around and develop "active eyes." If you notice commotion involving several students and you have no idea what is going on, this is a sign that you have not been monitoring closely enough.

When students are working on individual assignments, monitoring should be done by circulating around the classroom and checking each student's progress periodically. You will of course help students who request assistance; however, you should not just "chase hands." If you do, you will not be aware of the progress of *all* the students. It is very difficult to monitor student progress on assignments from your desk or from any other fixed location, so spend as little time as possible being stationary. If you must work at your desk for a time, get up periodically and circulate around the room to check on students' progress and to make sure that directions are being followed correctly. If you must spend a long period of time (for example, more than a minute or two) helping an individual student, avoid doing it at the student's desk unless you can monitor the rest of the class from that position. For instance, if the student's seat is in the middle of the room, half of the class will be behind you. In such a case call the student to your desk, to the front of the room, or to some other location from which you can easily see all the students. Finally, when you work at your desk or at any other location, don't let students congregate around the area. They will obstruct your views of the class, and they may distract students seated nearby. Instead, call students to you one at a time.

A technique for monitoring at the beginning of seatwork that is effective in getting everyone started is to begin the work as a whole-group activity. Have students get out the necessary materials (be sure to look for these on the students' desks), head their papers, and then do the first exercise, problem, or answer the first question under your direction. Check and discuss this first item with the class. This makes it easy for you to scan the room to be sure that everyone has begun and to determine whether students understand what to do.

A critical monitoring task is checking assignments. Collect them regularly and look them over even when students do the checking in class. Keep your grade book current so that you will be able to detect students who are doing poor work or who skip assignments. If you give a long-term assignment, be sure to check progress regularly. You may even wish to give a grade or assign points toward a grade at these progress checks.

CONSISTENCY

The dictum "Be Consistent" has been repeated more frequently than the Pledge of Allegiance. It is still worth some discussion, however, because its meaning is not always clear. In the classroom consistency means retaining the same expectations for behaviors that are appropriate or inappropriate in particular activities; it also means that these expectations apply to every student on all occasions. For example, if students are expected to work silently during seatwork activities on Monday, the same procedure is in effect for all students on Tuesday, Wednesday, and so on. Consistency also applies to the use of penalties. For example, if the penalty for tardy arrival to class is detention, the teacher makes sure that all tardy students receive the penalty and that this procedure is followed even on the days when it is inconvenient to administer it, or in spite of the pleading of individual students that an exception be made. Obvious inconsistency in the use of procedures or in the application of penalties will usually cause students to "test the limits" by not following the procedure or by repeating whatever behavior was to have evoked the penalty. These events can rapidly escalate and force the teacher either to abandon the procedure or to tolerate high levels of inappropriate behavior. Because neither outcome is desirable, it is best to avoid the problem by learning to be consistent in the first place. Of course, it is not possible to be totally consistent, as there will be occasions when the most reasonable course of action will be to make an exception to a rule or procedure. Thus, a deadline for an assignment may be extended when a student has a valid reason, or some procedures might be ignored during an emergency. Note that procedures that are used routinely for some activities but not for others are not inconsistent. For example, you may stipulate that no one leave their seats without permission during discussions or presentations but that during seatwork students are allowed to get materials, sharpen pencils, or turn in papers as needed without permission. As long as you have differentiated between the activities when you explain the procedures to the students, no problems should arise.

Undesirable inconsistency usually arises from three sources. First, the procedures or rules are not reasonable, workable, or appropriate. Second, the teacher fails to monitor students closely and does not detect inappropriate behavior. This gives the appearance of inconsistency when the teacher *does* detect misbehavior and tries to stop it. Finally, the teacher may not feel strongly enough about the procedure or rule to enforce it or to use the associated penalty. If you find yourself caught in an inconsistency that is becoming a problem, your alternatives are:

1.   Reteach the procedure to the class. Take a few minutes to discuss the problem with the class and to reiterate your desire that it be followed. Then enforce it.

2.   Modify the procedure and then reintroduce it.

3.   Abandon the procedure or consequence, and possibly substitute another in its place.

The alternative you choose depends on circumstances and on the importance of the component to your classroom management system.

PROMPT MANAGEMENT OF INAPPROPRIATE BEHAVIOR

Prompt handling of inappropriate behavior is important in avoiding its continuation and spread. Behaviors that you should be concerned about include lack of involvement in learning activities, prolonged inattention or work avoidance, and obvious violations of classroom rules and procedures. It is *not* a good idea to ignore such behavior: Prolonged inattention will make it difficult for the students both to learn and to be able to complete assignments; violations of rules and failure to follow procedures create many problems we have already discussed. These behaviors should be dealt with directly, but without overreaction. A calm, reasoned tone or approach will be more productive and less likely to lead to confrontation. The following alternatives are recommended.

Four Ways to Manage Inappropriate Behavior

1.   When the student is off task—that is, not working on an assignment—redirect his or her attention to the task: "Robert, you should be writing now." Or "Becky, the assignment is to complete all the problems on the page." Check the students' progress shortly thereafter to make sure they are continuing to work.

2.   Make eye contact with or move closer to the student. Use a signal, such as a finger to the lips or a head shake, to prompt the appropriate behavior. Monitor until the student complies.

3.   If the student is not following a procedure correctly, simply reminding the student of the correct procedure may be effective. You can either state the correct procedure or ask the student if he or she remembers it.

4.   Ask or tell the student to stop the inappropriate behavior. Then monitor until it stops and the student begins constructive activity.

Sometimes it is inconvenient or would interrupt an activity to use these procedures immediately. In such a case make a mental note of the misbehavior and continue the activity until a more appropriate time occurs. Then tell the student you saw what was occurring, and discuss what the appropriate behavior should have been.

The four procedures outlined above are easy to use, cause little interruption of class activities, and enable students to correct their behavior. However, if a student persists in the behavior, some other alternatives must be used. If the rest of the class is working and does not need your immediate attention, a brief talk with the student and/or assessing an appropriate penalty may be sufficient. If that doesn't settle the matter, or if an immediate conference isn't desirable or feasible, tell the student to wait after class to speak to you. If the student is being disruptive, send him or her to a time-out desk in another part of the room, or send the student to the hall. Then talk with the student when you have time. Your goal in discussing the problem behavior with the student is to make clear what the unacceptable behavior is and what the student should be doing, and then to obtain a commitment from the student for acceptable behavior. Some teachers like to have the student put the commitment in writing in a brief "contract" or "plan," specifying what he or she agrees to do, before the student is allowed to return to class. Note that these procedures apply to relatively moderate forms of misbehavior. More severe transgressions (for example, fighting or open defiance) are discussed later under "Special Problems."

When to Ignore

Some inappropriate behaviors are of such short duration or are so insignificant that they can be safely ignored. Indeed, to do otherwise would give them undesirable attention and interfere unnecessarily with the flow of the lesson or with your helping other students. You can ignore inappropriate behavior when it meets the following criteria:

1. It is of short duration and not likely to persist or spread,
2. It is a minor deviation, and
3. Reacting to it would interrupt a lesson or call attention to the behavior.

Examples of behaviors that meet these criteria include occasional callouts during discussions; brief whispering among students during a lesson; or short periods of inattentiveness, perhaps accompanied by visual wandering or daydreaming. There is no point in worrying about such trivial behaviors as long as they are not disruptive; they don't significantly affect student cooperation or involvement in learning activities. To attempt to react to them would consume too much of your energy, interrupt your lessons constantly, and detract from your classroom's climate.

SPECIAL PROBLEMS

Secondary students sometimes behave in ways that require measures other than the simple ones described in the preceding sections. Some of these behaviors include the following: rudeness toward the teacher, chronic avoidance of work, fighting, other aggressive behavior, and defiance or hostility toward the teacher. While these behaviors are not pleasant to contemplate, they are sometimes an inevitable result of close contact with up to 150 adolescents on a daily basis. Fortunately, few teachers encounter these behaviors in large amounts. Regardless of their frequency, you should be aware of ways to cope with them in the event they do occur.

Before discussing each type of problem, some general guidelines applicable to aggressive behaviors in general will be considered. You should think of coping with these behaviors in two phases: your immediate response and a long-range strategy. At the time you encounter the behavior, your immediate concern will generally be to bring it to a halt with a minimum of further disruption. Because these behaviors are annoying and frequently arouse anxiety or anger, you will need to be careful not to exacerbate the problem. Stay calm and avoid overreaction. You can tell the student how you feel, but avoid an argument or an emotional confrontation. You will then be in a better position to deal with the student. Long-range considerations are to prevent a recurrence of the behavior and to help the student learn a more constructive means of dealing with others. Preventing a recurrence of the behavior is best accomplished by (1) finding out what triggered the incident and dealing with the cause, if possible, and (2) having a predictable classroom environment, with reasonable and consistently used rules, procedures, and consequences. Such classrooms rarely have large amounts of these behaviors. Helping students acquire better behavior may require working with the students on an individual basis over a period of time. The extent to which this goal is feasible is of course limited by many factors, including your time constraints and the seriousness of the student's problem. Finally, other professionals such as a counselor, a special education resource teacher, or an assistant principal may be able to assist in dealing with chronic problems.

In the discussion below some suggestions for handling different types of behavior are presented.

Rudeness Toward the Teacher

This may take the form of sassy back talk, arguing, crude remarks, or gesturing. An important consideration with this type of behavior is not to overreact or argue with the student. Frequently this type of behavior is a means of getting attention either from you or from peers, so don't get trapped into a power struggle. Your response will depend to some extent on the degree of rudeness. In borderline cases the student may not even realize that a comment was offensive. A reasonable first reaction is to inform the student that the behavior is not acceptable and to refer to a general classroom rule such as "Respect others" or "Be polite." If the incident is repeated, or if the original comment was quite rude, then some type of penalty can be used. In the case of really obnoxious behavior that disrupts the class or that persists, the student can be sent to the school office and not allowed to return until he or she agrees to behave appropriately. Usually the school will have a standard policy for dealing with extreme cases, and you should use whatever procedures have been established.

Chronic Avoidance of Work

You may have students who frequently do not complete assigned work. Sometimes they fail to complete assignments early in the school year; more often a student will begin to skip assignments occasionally, and then with increasing regularity, until he or she is habitually failing to do the assigned work. This behavior can be minimized by an accountability system that clearly ties student work to grades (review Chapter Three for details). However, even in classrooms with a strong accountability system, some students still may avoid work.

It is much easier (and much better for the student) if you deal with this problem before the student gets so far behind that failure is almost certain. By catching the problem early, you are still able to provide some incentive (that is, passing the course) for the student getting back on track. In order to be in a position to take early action, you must collect and check student work frequently and also maintain good records. Then, when you note a student who has begun to miss assignments, you can talk with him or her to identify the problem. It is possible that the student is simply unable to do the work. If so, then you may be able to arrange appropriate assistance or modify the assignments for that student. It is also possible that the student feels overwhelmed by the assignments. In this case break up the assignments into parts, whenever possible. Have the student complete the first part of the assignment within a specified period of time (for example, five or ten minutes), then check to see that it has been done. A bonus of a few minutes of free time at the end of the period (for example, to sit quietly, read, do an enrichment activity, or help with a classroom chore) can be offered for completion of the portion within the time limit or for working steadily without prodding.

If ability is not the problem, then in addition to talking with the student, the following procedures can be used. Call the student's parents or guardian and discuss the situation. Often the home can supply the extra support needed to help motivate the student. Also, if the student participates in athletics or other extracurricular activities, the coaches or other supervising faculty may be able to support your efforts. Many schools have a system (for example, a weekly checklist) for monitoring academic progress of students involved in certain extracurricular activities. Finally, apply the consequence, usually a failing grade, of repeated neglect of work. There is no purpose served in softening the penalty because the student promises to do the work during the next grading period or because you think that he or she could do better by just working harder! Doing so teaches the student to avoid responsibility.

Fighting

This is rarely a classroom problem; usually it occurs in hallways or in other areas of the school. Whether or not to intervene directly will depend on your judgment as to whether you can do so without undue risk of injury. If you do not intervene directly, you should of course alert other teachers and administrators so that action can be taken. If you do intervene, try to do so with the assistance of one or several adults. It's hard to stop a fight by yourself, particularly when a crowd has gathered. Your school will undoubtedly have a procedure to deal with fighting, so you should familiarize yourself with what your responsibility is (for example, to file a report with the office). Typically students will be questioned by an assistant principal who will call the student's home, arrange a conference, and mete out any prescribed penalty, such as suspension.

"...and suddenly there were teachers
all over the place!"

Other Aggressive Behavior

Students engage in other types of aggressive behavior toward fellow students besides fighting, and it may occur in the classroom. Examples include name calling, overbearing bossiness or rudeness toward other students, and physically aggressive—but "playful"—pushing, shoving, or slapping. Such behavior should be treated in the same way as rudeness toward the teacher. Offending students should be told that such behavior is not acceptable, even if it is just "fooling around." It can easily escalate. Refer to whatever class rule fits the situation, such as "Respect others." Give no more than one warning and then assess an appropriate penalty. Students engaged in such behavior should be separated and seated apart if they give any indication of intending to persist.

Defiance or Hostility Toward the Teacher

This type of behavior is understandably very threatening, particularly when it occurs in front of other students. The teacher feels, and rightfully so, that if the student is allowed to get away with it, such behavior may continue, and other students will be more likely to react this way. The student, however, has provoked the confrontation, usually publicly, and backing down would cause a loss of face in front of peers. The best way to deal with such an event is to try to defuse it. This can be done by keeping it private and handling it individually with the student, if possible. If it occurs during a lesson and is not really extreme, deal with it by trying to depersonalize the event and avoid a power struggle. "This is taking time away from the lesson. I will discuss it with you in a few minutes when I have time." Then leave the student alone and give him or her a chance to calm down. Later, when you have time, have a private talk with the student and assess a penalty if it seems warranted. Should the student not accept the opportunity you have provided but rather press the confrontation further, you can instruct the student to leave the room and wait in the hall. After the student has had time to cool off, you can give your class something to do and discuss the problem privately with the student.

When presented with this type of behavior, you should try to stay objective. Don't engage in arguments with the student. Point out that the behavior was not acceptable and state the penalty clearly. Listen to the student's point of view, and if you are not sure how to respond, say that you will think about it and discuss it later.

In an extreme (and rare) case, the student may be totally uncooperative and refuse to keep quiet or to leave the room. If this happens, you can send another student to the office for assistance. In almost all cases, however, as long as you stay calm and refuse to get into a power struggle with the student, the student will take the opportunity to cool down.

SUGGESTED ACTIVITIES

Each of the two short paragraphs below describes a common problem situation in secondary classrooms. After reading one of the paragraphs, review the contents of this chapter and think about specific strategies you would recommend to the teacher. Discuss both problem cases with other teachers; then put together "brainstorming" lists of suggestions addressing each problem. Compare your lists with the suggestions in the activity key in Appendix B.

Problem A: Improving Class Behavior

Ms. Marcus is concerned because no matter how hard she tries to follow through with classroom behavior requirements, her students continue to call out, leave their seats, talk with their neighbors, and write notes. Within one class period, she wrote seven students' names on the board for talking, after having warned them several times to stop; she turned one boy's seat away from the class for clowning around and making other students giggle; she warned one girl twice about giving answers to other students who had been called on; and she threatened to keep two boys after school for shooting paper "basketballs" into the trash can. She decided that she needed to stop giving so many warnings before following through on consequences. What else would you suggest that Ms. Marcus do?

Problem B: "Problem" Students

Ms. Jones is especially concerned about two students. *Greg* does very little work, even when the teacher helps him get started and sees that he understands how to proceed. Greg tends to spend most of his time watching other students. He just shuffles his paper when told to get to work and shrugs when asked where his work is when it is due. *Joe*, on the other hand, manages to get most of his work done, but in the process he is constantly disruptive. He flirts with and teases the girls sitting around him, keeping them constantly giggling and competing for his attention. Joe makes wisecracks in response to almost everything Ms. Jones says. When confronted by her, he grins charmingly and responds with exaggerated courtesy, much to the delight of the rest of the class.

In her efforts to improve the boys' behavior, Ms. Jones has talked privately with both of them. She moved Greg to a desk close to her own to make it easier to watch him and keep him on task. She has moved Joe's desk away from those of his friends several times, but he seems able to stir up excitement wherever he sits. Despite Ms. Jones's efforts, these two students continue to pose particular problems. What else can she do?

CHAPTER SEVEN
ORGANIZING
AND CONDUCTING
INSTRUCTION

Just as good classroom management enhances learning by helping to create a good environment for teaching, so too does effective instruction contribute to a well-managed classroom. Good instruction aids management by keeping students involved in appropriate learning activities, and it helps prevent failure, frustration, boredom, and confusion. In this chapter we will describe aspects of instructional management that affect student involvement in lessons and that preserve as much time as possible for learning.

Two key aspects of instruction will be described: the management of activities within a class period and the organization and presentation of information. The discussion of activity management will focus on the way different components of a class period are chosen, sequenced, and paced. The section on presenting information will address the problem of conducting instruction in a clear, comprehensible manner. Although this chapter is not intended to substitute for the outlining of specific methods of teaching particular subjects, organizing and arranging activities and communicating information are basic to all content areas. Consequently, the ideas presented in this chapter will be helpful for managing instruction in whatever secondary subject you teach.

THE MANAGEMENT OF ACTIVITIES

The term *activity* describes organized behavior that the teacher and students engage in for a common purpose. Typical activities in secondary classes include discussions, recitations, presentations, seatwork, and checking, although this is by no means a complete list. Furthermore, activities do not always need to be content based. For example, beginning-of-period activities may be mainly procedural.

Activities are an important aspect of instructional planning—they consume time, and time is a precious commodity. Class periods are usually about an hour in length, so activities must be limited accordingly. Thus, given certain learning objectives, you will need to identify those activities that will most likely lead to attaining the objectives within the allotted period of time.

Activities are also selected, in part, on the basis of their potential for involving students in the lesson. This consideration suggests that several activities, rather than just one activity, be planned for a period, because in many secondary classes students' attention is difficult to maintain in the same activity for long periods of time. Activities that provide for student participation or that provide each student with an opportunity to practice or apply lesson content are also desirable; they help students learn the content, and they promote high levels of involvement in the lesson. To summarize, your task in instructional management is to select and arrange activities that result in high levels of student learning and involvement and that make good use of the available time.

Even though much of your daily planning for classes will focus on organizing activities, you should also keep in mind the broader perspective—your course as a whole. You need to know what knowledge and skills students are expected to acquire and what units, topics, or textbook chapters are typically included in the course. Examine the teachers' edition of your textbook and preview each major section, noting statements of overall objectives and the scope and sequence of content. Identifying reasonable expectations for your grade level will be helpful when deciding on course objectives and adequate coverage of topics. Other useful sources of information about appropriate content and reasonable expectations for students in particular age and grade levels may be found in school district or state education agency curriculum guides, courses and books on instructional methods in your subject, and yearbooks of national teachers' organizations in particular subject areas. Finally, your department chairperson, your instructional coordinator or supervisor, or other teachers in your subject area can provide helpful suggestions on course scope and topical sequence.

Some subjects, such as English/language arts and home economics, require extra effort when developing an overall plan of content organization. Contents of these subjects include several discrete areas and frequently use more than one textbook. For example, junior high school English components include writing, usage and grammar, literature, and spelling. In order to cover these diverse areas, it is common practice for three different textbooks to be used. In such a subject the teacher must determine an appropriate sequence for all components and decide how they will be merged into one course. If you teach one of these subjects, it will be particularly important for you to consult one or more of the information sources on curriculum mentioned in the preceding paragraph.

Types of Activities

The building blocks of a class period are briefly described below. Several concepts—critical to activity management—are then discussed: sequencing, pacing, and transitions.

Opening the period.   The chief concern in this activity is to help the students make an orderly transition into the classroom situation and be ready for the rest of the period, while the teacher handles administrative tasks such as the attendance check and helping previously absent students. We have described in Chapters Two and Five alternatives for structuring the opening, including the use of either academic "warm-ups" or an administrative routine with stated expectations for student behavior.

Checking classwork or homework.   In this activity students check their own work or exchange papers in order to check other students' work. The activity is appropriate only when the judgment as to the correctness of the work can easily be made. Checking provides quick feedback to students about their work and allows the teacher to identify and discuss common errors on assignments. Careful monitoring during checking is important to prevent cheating. Some teachers discourage cheating by requiring that checking be done with a different color ink than the assignment, with a pencil if the assignment was completed with ball point pen, or vice versa. When student checking is used frequently, you should collect and examine the students' papers, even when you record grades in class. This procedure will enable you to keep abreast of student progress and problems.

Recitation.   This activity is a question-and-answer sequence in which the techer asks questions, usually of a factual nature, and accepts or corrects student responses. This sequence of question/answer/ evaluation is repeated frequently, with many students being asked to respond until a body of content has been covered. In effect, a recitation is a form of checking, done orally. It can be used to provide practice, quickly review content, or check student understanding of a previous lesson or assigned reading. It can also be used to review spelling words, vocabulary definitions in any subject, or other verbal learning such as occurs in language classes.

Content development.   In this activity the teacher presents new information, elaborates or extends a concept or principle, conducts a demonstration, shows how to perform a skill, or describes how to solve a problem. During content development activities the teacher's questions are used to check student understanding and to maintain involvement. They also encourage students to contribute to the steps in problem solving, to apply concepts or principles, or to analyze the ideas being presented. In addition to questioning for comprehension, it is often a good idea to obtain work samples or other student demonstrations of the skills being taught during content development activities. Important skills for effective content development are described later under "Clarity."

Discussion.   In most secondary school classes, discussions are conducted as teacher-led, whole-class activities. The purpose of using discussion is to encourage students to evaluate events, topics, or results; to clarify the basis for their judgments; and to become aware of other points of view. Sometimes discussions are begun with a recitation activity in which the "facts" of the content to be discussed are reviewed. Compared to a recitation however, discussion questions are more likely to elicit student judgments and opinions, and teachers are less likely to evaluate the students' responses directly. Instead, students are encouraged to examine their opinions and beliefs and to understand other perspectives. The teacher's role then becomes one of clarifying and using student ideas rather than evaluating their correctness. When using a discussion format, careful planning of questions is needed. Students should also be made aware of your ground rules for participation (for example, raise hands, listen carefully, respect each person's right to express himself or herself). Few secondary classes, especially at the middle or junior high level, can sustain a discussion for very long, so plan short ones (for example, ten minutes) until you have an idea of what you and your classes can handle.

Seatwork.   In this activity, also known as classwork, students engage in assignments that provide practice or review of previously pres-

"You mean we have to process all that data?"

ented material. Often that portion of the seatwork assignment not completed in class becomes a homework assignment, unless the materials or resources needed to finish it are available only in the classroom. (Procedures for seatwork have been discussed in Chapter Two, and the reader should refer back if additional review is needed.) Seatwork is more valuable for consolidating or applying prior learning through practice than for learning *new* content. For that reasons, and also because it is difficult to maintain student involvement for a long period of time in seatwork activities, we strongly urge you to avoid devoting large portions of class periods to seatwork. A rule of thumb would be to devote no more time to seatwork than is allocated to content development activities each day.

Small group work.   In this activity two or more students work together. This activity might be used for drills on new vocabulary words or spelling, work on a laboratory activity in a science or homemaking class, reviewing for a test in any subject, preparing group reports, or discussing an issue or specific topic in social studies. Small groups work best with secondary students when objectives are clear and when steps or procedures for achieving them are understood by the students. Careful monitoring of the small groups is also needed so that you can be sure they are on track and can provide assistance when needed.

Closing.   The goal of this procedural activity is to bring the period to an end in an orderly manner, with students ready to pass to the next class, leaving your room in good condition for your next period. Teachers usually give students a warning before the bell is to ring so that students have enough time to put materials away and get their own things ready. Other procedures for the closing activity were discussed in Chapter Two.

In the preceding discussion each activity was treated as a discrete event; in practice, activities are often combined. Thus, a teacher may combine recitation and content development activities or discussion and recitation. If you find that using some combination of activities is more suitable for your lesson goals than planning separate activities, by all means pursue the lesson structure that helps accomplish your objectives more effectively.

Choosing and Arranging Activities

The center stage of instruction is occupied by *content development* activities, because it is during these that much new learning takes place. However, all class periods include other activities, and so one must plan an appropriate sequence for them. A commonly observed sequence of activities in secondary school classrooms is as follows:

Opening routine
Checking
Content development
Seatwork
Closing

Advantages of this sequence are that it has a minimum number of transition points, allows checking and feedback of the prior day's work, provides for the presentation of new material, and has a practice or application period. As mentioned earlier, we recommend that the content development activity be allocated at least as much time as the seatwork activity, and preferably more.

A disadvantage of the preceding sequence is that it does not easily allow for the presentation of different topics within the same period, and it also requires that the content be amenable to presentation and practice in two lengthy segments. A common variation of the sequence that accommodates more than one type of content or more complex content is

Opening
Checking
First content development activity
First seatwork activity
Checking
Second content development activity
Second seatwork activity
Closing

This sequence can be used when two different types of content must be taught within the same period and the teacher wants to provide a period of practice using classwork exercises following each content development activity. The sequence can also be used when a complex lesson is separated into two phases of content development, each followed by seatwork. Subdividing new content into two different parts with an intervening practice activity will help students consolidate learning from the first part before they are asked to contend with the new learning required in the second part of the lesson. It also allows the teacher to check student understanding and provide prompt feedback. Another advantage of this sequence is that student attention will usually be easier to maintain when individual activities are divided into shorter segments. A disadvantage of this sequence is that it produces more transition points and may be more difficult to manage. However, as long as the teacher is sensitive to the need to manage these transitions, the lesson format can be a useful one. (Note: A case study at the end of the chapter illustrates a lesson in which several content development-seatwork cycles are used effectively.)

Pacing

In content development activities pacing refers to the fit between the rate of presentation of information and the students' ability to comprehend it. In other activities pacing refers to the time students have to complete tasks. While no hard and fast rules prescribing how to pace instruction can be given, two major guidelines can be suggested. First, adequate time must be available for the planned activities. Second, the teacher must be aware of student comprehension so that the rate of presentation or task implementation can be modified when necessary. Preserving adequate time for each activity requires good planning, an awareness of time during the lesson, and self-discipline. Staying abreast of student comprehension requires careful monitoring of student progress, especially during content development activities. Frequent questions, written work samples, and demonstrations of skills by students should be used as checks on understanding.

Transitions

The interval between any two activities is a transition. In addition, the beginning and ending of periods are transitions. Several management problems can occur at these times, including long delays before starting the next activity and higher levels of inappropriate or disruptive student behavior. Some of the causes of transition problems include a lack of readiness by the teacher or the students for the next activity, unclear student expectations about appropriate behavior during transitions, and faulty procedures. Efficient transitions are important for several reasons: Much time can be wasted during poor transitions, and misbehavior can spill over into subsequent activities. Examples of transition problems are listed below along with some suggested ways of correcting these problems.

TRANSITION PROBLEM

SUGGESTED SOLUTION

Students talk loudly at the beginning of the period. The teacher is interrupted while checking attendance, and the start of content activities is delayed.

Establish a beginning-of-period routine and make expectations for student behavior at the beginning of the period clear.

Students socialize too much during transitions, especially after a seatwork assignment has been given, but before they've begun working on it. Many students do not start their seatwork activity for several minutes.

Be sure students know what the assignment is; post it where they can see it easily. Work as a whole class on the first several seatwork exercises so that all students begin the lesson successfully and at the same time. Then watch what students do during the transition and hurry them along when needed.

Students stop working well before the end-of-period bell; they then engage in excessive talking and mess up the room.

An end-of-period routine should be established: Students work until the teacher gives a signal and then they clean up around their desks before being dismissed.

Whenever the teacher attempts to move the students from one activity into another, a number of students don't make the transition but continue working on the preceding activity. This delays the start of the next activity or results in confusion.

The teacher should give the class notice a few minutes *before* an activity is scheduled to end. At the end of the activity, students should be told to put all the materials from that activity away and get out any materials needed for the next activity. The teacher should monitor the transition to make sure that all students complete it; the next activity should not be started until students are ready.

While the teacher gives directions during a transition, many students do not pay attention. They continue to put their materials away or get out new materials.

Don't try to give instructions *during* a transition, except to individual students. Instead, give the whole class instructions before the transition begins. Don't begin explaining the new activity or presenting content until everyone is ready and listening.

A few students always seem to be slowpokes during transitions, delaying the rest of the class.

Don't wait for one or two students and hold up the rest of the class. Go ahead and start, but be sure to monitor the dawdlers in later transitions in order to find out why they are having trouble. Then give them individual feedback and close supervision.

Students frequently leave their seats to socialize, come up to the teacher to ask questions, or attempt to get a bathroom permit,

Define appropriate behavior during transitions more clearly and explain the rationale for limiting student behavior during these

TRANSITION PROBLEM	SUGGESTED SOLUTION
go to the trash basket, or wander around the room during transitions.	times. Monitor students and be sure procedures are established to handle out-of-seat behavior.
The teacher delays the beginning of activities to look for materials, finish attendance reporting, pass back or collect papers, or chat with individual students while the rest of the students wait.	The teacher needs to have all materials ready, and once transitions begin, the teacher should avoid doing anything that interferes with his or her ability to monitor and direct students.

CLARITY[1]

The preceding items summarize the major problems that occur in classrooms at and around transition times. If you should find yourself having difficulty keeping control, or if you feel that your class is wasting time during transitions, a look at the suggested solutions may prove helpful.

Communicating information and directions in a clear, comprehensible manner is a teaching skill of great importance. Clear instruction helps students learn faster and more successfully; it also helps students understand your directions and expectations for behavior more readily. Although clarity is important in all classroom activities, it is crucial during content development, when nearly all new subject matter is introduced and taught. Thus, this section will focus mainly on ways to improve clarity during this critical portion of the period.

Clear instruction results from several factors: the organization of information into a coherent sequence, the use of an adequate number of good illustrations or examples, precision and concreteness of expression, keeping in touch with student comprehension, and providing enough practice to ensure mastery. The following chart illustrates some of the many ways teachers can be both clear and unclear in their instruction.

POOR CLARITY	BEING CLEAR
1. Communicating Lesson Objectives	
Not describing the lesson's purpose or what students are expected to learn	Stating goals or major objectives at the beginning of the lesson
Not calling students' attention to main points, ideas, or concepts	Telling students what they will be accountable for knowing or doing
	Emphasizing major ideas as they are presented
	Reviewing key points or objectives at the end of the lesson

[1]The authors appreciate the suggestions of Barak Rosenshine for the organization and content of this section.

POOR CLARITY	BEING CLEAR
2. Presenting Information Systematically	
Presenting information out of sequence; skipping important points or backtracking	Outlining the lesson sequence and sticking to it
Inserting extraneous information, comments, or trivia into the lesson	Sticking to the topic; holding back on complexities until the main idea is developed
Moving from one topic to another without warning	Summarizing previous points; clearly delineating major transitions between ideas or topics
Presenting too much complex information at once or giving directions too quickly	Breaking complex content into manageable portions or steps; giving step-by-step directions, checking for understanding before proceeding
Not leaving sufficient time to cover each aspect of the lesson thoroughly	Maintaining an efficient pace in early activities so that ample time remains for later ones
3. Avoiding Vagueness	
Presenting concepts without concrete examples	Providing a variety of apt examples
Using overly complex vocabulary	Using words students understand; defining new vocabulary terms
Overusing negative phrases (e.g., not all insects, not many people, not very happy)	Being specific and direct (e.g., the beetles, one third of the people, enraged, discouraged)
Being ambiguous or indefinite: maybe, perhaps, sort of correct, more or less right, you know, right most of the time, not always	Being specific, precise, referring to the concrete object, stating what is and is not correct and why
4. Checking for Understanding	
Assuming everyone understands, or simply asking, "Does everyone understand?" or "Does anyone have any questions?"; then proceeding without verification	Asking questions or obtaining work samples to be *sure* students are ready to move on
Moving to the next topic because time is short or because no students ask questions	Asking students to summarize main points to verify comprehension
	Reteaching unclear parts
Not calling on slower students; relying on feedback from a few volunteers only	Systematically checking everyone's understanding
5. Providing for Practice and Feedback	
Not assigning classwork or homework	Being sure students have adequate practice so that critical objectives are mastered
Giving assignments that cover only a portion of the learning	Reviewing assignments to be sure that all of the lesson's skills and concepts are reinforced
Not checking, reviewing, or discussing students' assigned work	Checking work regularly, reexplaining needed concepts, reteaching when appropriate

As the preceding examples illustrate, teachers can do many things to enhance (or detract from) the clarity of lessons. Following are some specific suggestions that can be applied to different aspects of your lessons and their planning.

Planning.   Organize the parts of your lesson into a coherent sequence. If the lesson is complex, write down the main components. Review the unit and lesson in the teachers' edition of your textbook(s). Pay careful attention to suggestions for lesson development and activities. Study the exercises, questions, problems and so on, provided in the textbook and decide which items would provide appropriate review of lesson objectives. Note examples, demonstrations, and key questions and activities to use in developing the main concepts. If some items in the seatwork assignment go well beyond the lesson scope, don't assign them as classwork or homework until you can teach the necessary content; or, if the content is not essential and you do not plan to teach it later, assign such items for enrichment or for extra credit.

Try to anticipate problems students may encounter in the lesson or assignments. Check for new terms and be ready to define them and present examples. Do some of the classwork or homework assignment yourself to uncover hurdles students will face. You can then build into your lesson some helpful hints or extra emphasis in these areas.

Presenting new content.   If students understand where a lesson is going, they are more likely to be there with you at the end. Tell students what the lesson objectives are, either at the beginning of or during the activity. If the lesson is at all complex, give students an outline to help them follow its organization. Displaying the topical sequence helps organize the content for the students and provides a road map to keep them on course.

As you present a lesson, stay with the planned sequence unless an obvious change is needed. Avoid needless digressions, interruptions, or tangential information. Inserting irrelevant information into a lesson only confuses students about what they are expected to learn. Displaying key concepts, new terms, major points, and other critical information on the overhead transparency screen or writing them on the chalkboard will underscore their importance; and, if students are required to take notes, the display will guide the information students record.

Presentation should be as focused and concrete as possible. Use examples, illustrations, demonstrations, physical props, charts, and other means of providing substance and dimension to abstractions in the lesson.

Reprinted by permission of Tribune Company Syndicate, Inc.

Avoid the vague expressions and verbal time fillers that, at best, communicate little information and make presentations difficult to follow.

Checking for understanding. Find out whether students understand a presentation *during* the lesson rather than later. As content development activities unfold, students can be asked questions to verify their comprehension of main points. You can also ask students to provide a written response to key questions and then check some or all of the students either orally or by examining the written work. Asking all students to demonstrate comprehension at several points during a presentation not only allows you to verify their progress, but keeps students more involved in the lesson.

Another way to check student understanding at the end of a presentation is to conduct an oral recitation on the lesson's main points. Do this by asking a series of questions that recapitulate the lesson sequence and its major concepts. Involve many students in these question-and-answer sequences so that you can identify the overall level of understanding in the class and reteach what has not been satisfactorily learned.

SUGGESTED ACTIVITIES

The two short paragraphs below describe problems two teachers are experiencing with organizing and presenting instruction. After reading each paragraph, review the relevant sections in Chapter Seven and in other parts of this book and decide what strategies would be helpful in overcoming the problem. You might also use each case as a basis for a group discussion and generate a list of many possible solutions or strategies. Compare your list with that included in the key in Appendix B.

PROBLEM A

In Ms. Carpenter's class there almost always seem to be some students who don't understand presentations or assignments and who need a lot of reexplanation. While she is lecturing, she is continually asked a lot of questions by students about what they should write in their notes. When an in-class assignment is made, she finds herself answering many questions about information she has just covered in the lecture. Sometimes she has to reexplain parts of the lesson to the whole class. As a result, there is often not enough time to complete activities before the end of the period. In an attempt to avoid the problems associated with note taking, she decides to write important information on the chalkboard during the lecture. What else can Ms. Carpenter do?

PROBLEM B

Mr. Miller feels that too much time is wasted in his ninth-grade class while students get settled after class changes, get supplies ready, or change from one activity to another. While the teacher deals with students' problems, makeup work, or questions at the beginning of class, students talk and begin to play around or wander. It then takes some time to get their attention and get class started. Also, in activity changes during the class period, students sometimes delay activities while they sharpen pencils or borrow supplies. Trading papers to check work in class usually results in some confusion.

Mr. Miller has already spoken with his class about the problem and has reminded them of the rules for sharpening pencils immediately upon arrival and taking seats before the bell. He tries to enforce these two rules, but he is also required to monitor the hall. What else can he do to cut down on wasted time?

CASE STUDY 7-1:
EFFECTIVE INSTRUCTIONAL MANAGEMENT
IN AN ENGLISH CLASS

Description	Comments
When the bell rings, all the students are in their seats except for two who are distributing journal notebooks. When students receive their notebooks, they begin writing on the day's topic, which is written on the chalkboard. During this time Mr. Evans checks attendance and confers with a few students about procedural matters.	The *opening activity* (5 minutes) helps the students make the transition into the room while the teacher takes care of administrative chores.

CASE STUDY 7-1: (*CONT.*)

Description

Comments

About 30 seconds before the end of the opening activity, Mr. Evans tells the students how much time remains; at the end of the opening activity, students pass their journal noteboks to the front of their row, where they are collected by Mr. Evans.

Students are given notice of the end of the activity and the upcoming transition.

He tells the class, "Please get out your grammar book and open up to page 57. Also, get out your notes from yesterday on the parts of speech—the definition page." He then reviews the assignment from yesterday on identifying *idea* nouns. The assigment was to make a list of at least twenty of these nouns. The teacher calls on several students to read their lists. After the students have read their lists, the teacher comments and gives feedback to students.

Recitation (5 minutes) In this activity the preceding day's assignment is reviewed.

After collecting the papers Mr. Evans explains that in today's lesson students will continue their study of nouns. They will learn how to distinguish between proper and common nouns and they will learn how to change from one noun type to the other. He tells them, "Knowing the difference is important because you must always capitalize proper nouns. Being able to change from one to the other will help you recognize which is which." He then explains proper nouns, reads the definition, and says, "The key word in this is *particular*." He also emphasizes that the proper noun is always capitalized. "In the definition of common noun, the key word is *any*." Mr. Evans then illustrates proper and common nouns and presents numerous examples to students, asking them to make the correct classification. He also states, "On your notes on the parts of speech page, let's copy these the definitions for common noun and proper noun." Mr. Evans gives instructions, "Underline the word that is being defined in your notes so that you can find it easily." The teacher goes around the room checking as the class works on copying the definitions.

Content development (14 minutes).

Next, students are directed to get out paper, draw a line down the middle, and copy proper and common nouns into the columns from an exercise in the textbook. Students work on the assignment as the teacher circulates and checks progress.

This *seatwork activity* (6 minutes) provides practice with the word discrimination presented in the previous activity.

After several minutes Mr. Evans stops the class and goes through the first part of the list, asking students how they classified each noun. He then summarizes what they have done to this point and says, "Let's turn the page."

Recitation (5 minutes) allows checking and feedback before proceeding.

Mr. Evans then describes how proper nouns can be converted to common nouns, and vice versa. He provides several examples and converts them. He then presents more examples and solicits student response and analysis. Mr. Evans then gives each row a different sentence to work on, and he calls on different students to read their sentences with the

Content development (13 minutes). In this segment a new concept is introduced, building on the previously presented material. Students are given examples

CASE STUDY 7-1: (*CONT.*)

Description

Comments

nouns converted. When the students read the sentence, the teacher repeats the answer to the class and comments on the sentence.

Students are then given a homework assignment, to be started in class, providing further practice distinguishing proper and common nouns and transforming one to the other. Mr. Evans monitors students during the remainder of the period, providing assistance as needed.

to work on in class, and all students can benefit from the teacher's comments.

Seatwork (7 minutes).

CHAPTER EIGHT
MANAGING SPECIAL GROUPS

Although the classroom management principles and guidelines discussed in previous chapters generalize to most classroom settings, classroom management is, of course, affected by the characteristics of the students making up a class. The ages, academic ability levels, goals, interests, and home backgrounds of students have an impact on their classroom behavior. Consequently, effective teachers adjust their managerial and instructional practices to meet the needs of different groups of students. Two groups that frequently present some special challenges are very heterogeneous classes and low-ability, or remedial-level, classes. This chapter presents some information and suggestions that, combined with the principles described in previous chapters, will help you organize and manage these two kinds of classes successfully.

TEACHING HETEROGENEOUS CLASSES

Many secondary school classrooms contain students with a very wide range of entering achievement levels. For example, a heterogeneous eighth-grade English class may include some students who score at fourth-grade levels on reading and language usage achievement tests and other students with grade equivalent scores of eleventh grade or higher. In junior high mathematics classes, students' entering achievement levels may be spread across five or more grade levels. Required science and social studies courses often present extremes of student heterogeneity, with students varying greatly in their entering achievement levels in reading comprehension, mathematical reasoning, and content knowledge. Of course, any class is to some extent heterogeneous: No two students are alike. Ideally, every individual student should receive instruction tailored to his or her needs, abilities, interests, and learning style. In practice, the pupil/teacher ratio in most secondary schools makes large group instruction the most common and efficient means of teaching the standard curriculum. However, in very heterogeneous classes a whole-class assignment may be unchallenging or repetitious for some students and too difficult for the very low achievers. Students who are bored or frustrated are not likely to stay involved in activities, and inappropriate or disruptive behavior may result. Extreme heterogeneity may, therefore, have an impact on the management of student behavior as well as on instruction. Attempting to cope with heterogeneity by using many different assignments, providing an individualized, self-paced program, or using small group instruction extensively in secondary classrooms increases the complexity of classroom management, requires a great deal of planning and preparation, and may require instructional materials that are not readily available. Rather than completely altering their instructional approach, many effective teachers provide for different levels of student ability by supplementing their whole-class instruction with limited use of special materials, activities, assignments, and small group work. The following instructional procedures will help you cope successfully with very heterogeneous classes.

Assessing Entering Achievement

The first step in planning for instruction in a heterogeneous class is to gather information about students' entering achievement levels and skills in areas that will affect their ability to succeed in your classroom. You can get this information by investigating existing test scores, administering pretests, and carefully assessing student performance on classwork in the first weeks of school. Results of achievement or aptitude testing from the previous school year may be available through the counselors' office. Examining these scores will give you an idea of the extent of differences in your classes and will identify outlying students. Of course, achievement test scores are less than perfect indicators, and scores may not be available for all your students, so you will probably want to consider existing test data in conjunction with your own pretest(s) or informal assessments. To select an appropriate pretest, consult with the department chairperson, with other teachers in your academic department, or with the curriculum coordinator or supervisor in your district. The teachers' edition of your textbook may include a recommended pretest. If a prepared test is not available, you may have to prepare your own, based on content from the first part of the textbook your students will use.

You can also obtain useful information about student ability levels in your classes by carefully examining students' classwork at the beginning of the year. For example, in many courses the ability to follow a lecture and take good notes is important. It is a good idea, therefore, to present a short "typical" lecture at the beginning of the year, telling students ahead of time that you will be collecting and checking their notes. This assessment will help you identify students who are likely to need special assistance and monitoring during content development activities. Similarly, requiring that students read a short section of the text, outline it, and answer some comprehension questions in class will give you an idea of the range of students' abilities to learn from the textbook you will be using.

Modifying Whole-Group Instruction

Once you have information abut how heterogeneous your classes are, you can plan appropriate adjustments of your instruction. First, consider ways that you can accommodate different student needs simply by modifying your whole-class activities. For example:

Participation. During class discussions, recitations, or content development activities, be careful to include *all* students. Use some system (for example, going up and down the rows) to be sure each student has opportunities to participate frequently. Guard against the tendency to focus only on the higher- (or lower-) achieving students, allowing them to set the pace for the lesson.

Accountability procedures. In very heterogeneous classes carefully planned and implemented student accountability procedures become especially important. You need to get information daily about how all students are performing, and students will benefit from frequent individual feedback. Your accountability system should accommodate extra-credit or enrichment assignments, and it must also be designed so that lower-achieving students who work diligently and make progress can make a satisfactory grade.

Seating arrangement.   If you have one or two students who are especially likely to have trouble with whole-class assignments, place these students where you can easily keep an eye on them during instruction and seatwork. As soon as you have given seatwork instructions to the whole class and have monitored to ensure that students have begun work, check with the slower student(s) privately, either to go over instructions again or to modify the assignment, as needed. If there are more than two such students, however, treat them as a small group when giving supplemental instructions.

Flexible assignments.   Include some classroom activities that can be done together as a whole class but at different levels by different students. Use a grading or credit system that emphasizes individual student progress rather than competition among students. Some examples of such activities include projects or reports, reading assignments of varying difficulty, and fluency writing exercises in which students write for a specified period of time on an assigned topic, trying to increase the number of words they can generate each day. Other assignments that can be challenging to students at many different achievement levels include various composition and creative thinking assignments with open-ended directions such as: List all the Spanish-*ar* verbs you can think of; Name as many protein foods (or mammals, or words with EAT in them, or nations, and so on) as you can. When assigning research papers or projects, provide some *choice* of topics, or assign topics to students individually, adjusting the difficulty of the topic and the amount of structure you pr ovide according to student ability.

Supplementary materials.   Supplement whole-group instruction by providing enrichment materials for high-achieving students and remedial (review or practice) materials for lower-achieving students. These mater ials can be used as the basis for regular, differentiated assignments or as extra-credit options. To differentiate class or homework assignments, plan a core or basic assignment that all students must complete. Then provide an additional part or parts that are either optional (for example, those seeking an A grade) or required of different groups (for example, different spelling groups). Begin building a collection of supplementary materials by examining workbooks and texts from other grade levels, borrowing from other teachers and your curriculum coordinators, and reading professional journals and magazines in your content area.

Enrichment or extra-credit material for students who finish classwork early should be work related and should not distract other students. Avoid free-time activities that are so attractive that slower-working students feel deprived or are tempted to stop or rush through their work. Provide supplementary reading materials at a variety of reading levels. Set up a system for giving credit, feedback, or recognition for completion of enrichment activities.

Peer tutoring.   Another way to deal with student heterogeneity in the classroom is to encourage peer tutoring and cooperation among students on some assignments or projects. You may sometimes ask specific students to serve as tutors or helpers during class. Because mixed-ability work groups provide a good opportunity for students to help and to learn from each other, it is a good idea for you to carefully assign students to work groups or teams rather than just letting them choose their friends. (See discussion of group work in Chapter Seven.) Intergroup competition and group grades or rewards can provide additional motivation for students to cooperate. Research has shown that working in mixed-ability teams can benefit both higher-and lower-ability students in many subject areas.

Small Group Instruction

In some classes or in some content areas, the preceding suggestions for modifying or supplementing whole-class instruction may not be adequate to solve the heterogeneity "problem." In these classes teachers might need to use small group instruction, forming relatively homogeneous subgroups. This commonly occurs in reading courses, in English classes for spelling instruction, or in mathematics classes where some students lack skills in basic operations necessary to go on to more advanced work. In many subjects small group instruction might be used as a temporary measure with a group of students who have failed to pass a criterion-referenced test of material that is a prerequisite to subsequent units. The following are some examples of how small group instruction might be conducted in secondary classes.

> An eighth-grade English teacher uses small group instruction for spelling only. She has three groups: six students using spelling materials at the fourth-grade level, sixteen at the eighth-grade level, and five using advanced materials to prepare them for interscholastic competition. After opening class the teacher goes over general seatwork directions with the whole class. Seatwork directions are written on the board. They include one or two assignments (such as journal writing) that students can do without any further explanation from the teacher. Groups two and three begin seatwork while the teacher meets with the first spelling group for content development and more seatwork directions. The teacher then meets with group two for checking and content development and gives them another assignment. She checks on the first group again before moving to content development with group three. In the time remaining in the period, after she finishes with group three, she gives individual help to students and monitors seatwork.

An eight-grade math teacher uses whole-class instruction for approximately the first half of the lessons in each chapter. Then students are divided into two groups: one containing six students and one with twenty-two students. The smaller group, which has students who are very deficient in math skills, uses a supplementary workbook covering essentially the same content and receives a second sequence of presentation, review, and practice similar to the material previously covered. The larger group continues in the textbook chapter until it has been completed.

Athough small group instruction can help cope with extreme heterogeneity, it presents more problems than modifying whole class instruction. Small group instruction makes classroom management and organization more difficult. It also requires more extensive planning and more materials—important considerations when you must prepare for five different class sections. Monitoring student behavior and work is more difficult because you are instructing the groups most of the period. Another important consideration is that when small group instruction is used, students frequently spend relatively short periods of time interacting with you in content development and long periods of time in seatwork. Consequently, seatwork assignments have to be planned so that students will be able to do them with little assistance from the teacher. Despite all these problems, small group instruction may sometimes be necessary to meet your students' needs, and it can be managed well with careful attention to instructional planning and classroom procedures. Some of the procedures you will have to decide on and explain to your students, should you use small group instruction, are listed below.

Location of group.   Wherever you plan to meet, be sure that the location allows you to watch the rest of the class while you are working with the small group. Other considerations include minimizing distractions and making efficient use of classroom space and time.

Decide whether to rearrange student seating according to group or, if you have space in your room, whether you wish to set up a group instruction area. Rearranging seats by group has the advantage of eliminating student movement when you change groups; *you* move from one group to the other—the students needn't leave their desks to move to the group area. Also, you may be able to plan small group seating so that each group is close to a different board, screen, or display area for assignments and to different storage areas (for example, bookshelves) for materials. A disadvantage of rearranging seats according to small group assignment is that it may have the effect of segregating students by achievement level and emphasizing differences among students. A good alternative, if you have the classroom space and workable numbers of students in each of your small groups, is to set up a table for small group instruction at one end of your room.

Materials.　You will have to plan for and obtain materials and supplies for each group and set up files or other storage facilities.

Student movement.　If you are able to set up a small group instruction area to which you can call students, you will have to decide what procedures, rules, and signals you will use for student movement into and out of the group. Smooth and efficient transitions will depend on your explaining these procedures clearly and seeing that students follow them.

Out-of-group procedures.　Before using group work you will need to communicate your expectations for students not in the group. For example:

Will students be allowed to whisper or talk, or must they maintan silence?

Under what circumstances may they leave their seats?

What should they do if they need assistance on the assignment and you are not available?

What should they do when they finish their work?

TEACHING LOW-ABILITY CLASSES

In many secondary schools, especially in core academic subjects, students are assigned to classes on the basis of standardized test scores, academic record, teacher recommendations, diagnostic placement tests, or some combination of these factors. This process of homogeneous ability grouping or tracking results in the formation of several sections of a subject (for example, high, average, and low sections) or, at least, in special remedial classes for students deficient in basic skills. Such grouping practices are carried out on the assumption that they help schools provide instruction that meets the needs of all students. Many teachers and other educators believe that teaching and learning are more efficient when the range of ability in a class is not too great. Unfortunately, concentrating lower-ability students in homogeneous groups often exacerbates management problems. When teaching a lower-ability class, poor classroom management and organization can result in a classroom climate in which *any* student would have difficulty learning. It *is* possible, however, to manage low-ability classes effectively, and to maintain student involvement in learning activities, with little disruption. When such classes are effectively managed, students can make progress in the subject and complete the course with positive attitudes. Most of these students will do their work if they have a reasonable chance of success, and they will pay attention and cooperate with the teacher. However, obtaining good results with a low-ability class is not an easy job. It requires extra effort both in managing behavior and in organizing instruction. The following paragraphs describe how to use that effort efficiently.

Learner Characteristics

Students in low-ability or remedial classes usually are achieving two or more grade levels below average students for their grade and age group. Their grades in the subject usually have been low in the past, and some may have failed the subject in a previous year. These students bring with them more than their share of problems, some resulting from their lower achievement and some contributing to lower achievement. For example, absence and tardiness are often higher in such classes. The completion rate for assignments, particularly for homework, is likely to be lower than in "average" classes. Many low-achieving students are likely to view grades as arbitrary, failing to see a connection between their classwork and homework and the grades they receive in a course. Frequent failure in school in the past has caused some of these students to become very discouraged; and they may react by giving up easily or by fighting back. Teachers may encounter these reactions in the extremes of apathy, belligerence, or clowning around in class. Some of these students will be very poor readers, which will cause them problems in all subject areas. Others may have poor memory abilities. Most have poor study

"I'm an underachiever....
What's your racket?"

skills (for example, in taking notes, outlining, being organized and methodical, pacing efforts on long-term assignments). Maintaining attention for long periods of time is often difficult, particularly when encountering a demanding or frustrating task.

When considering these general characteristics, two important things should be kept in mind. First, a "homogeneous" low-ability class is not, of course, homogeneous at all. Such a class will contain students with a range of achievement levels, academic aptitudes, other talents, learning handicaps, goals and aspirations, attitudes toward school, and family backgrounds. Avoid making too many assumptions about individual students just because they have been placed in a "low" class. Second, the above description of general characteristics of students at low academic levels might be interpreted as a list of reasons why teaching low-ability classes effectively is difficult (or impossible). It is not intended as such. Instead, *it is intended as a description of needs that should be addressed by the management and organization plan for such a class.* These general characteristics of low-ability classes suggest some special considerations with regard to monitoring student behavior and work, establishing classroom procedures and rules, grading and accountability procedures, and organizing and presenting instruction.

Establishing Your Management System

In low-ability classes, particularly in the lower secondary grades, extra class time and attention may be required to *teach* students classroom procedures, rules, and routines at the beginning of the year. There may be more absences, shorter student attention spans, less ability to remember, and more testing of limits in such classes than in other class sections. Consequently, give extra attention to explaining, demonstrating, reviewing, and reminding students about your expectations; do not limit presentation, review, and feedback to only the first day or two of school. Plan to introduce and reinforce classroom procedures and routines gradually and methodically. Do not assume that students understand everything the first time you explain it. Question them, provide practice, and give them feedback. A "fun" written quiz on classroom procedures, routines, and requirements at the end of the first week of classes might be helpful. The following example illustrates how one junior high school teacher devoted part of class time throughout the first two weeks of school to establish her management system in a low-ability English class. After the first several weeks of school, the class was task oriented and functioned smoothly.

On the first day of school, a Monday, Ms. Evans spent about twenty minutes discussing school and class rules with students in her low-ability section. She described the rationale for each rule, and she explained the consequences of breaking rules. She also described a reward system for students who avoided detention hall during each six-week grading period. The discussion the first day was limited to basic school and class rules and procedures. Ms. Evans also described the routine to be used by the students at the beginning of class each day. She also told students what materials to bring to class, and she explained procedures they would use to turn in classwork.

On the second day of class, Ms. Evans devoted about twenty-one minutes to presenting additional procedures and reviewing some from the first day. As students entered the class, the teacher reminded them of the opening routine. After roll call she described and demonstrated the correct form for heading the daily assignment paper, and she circulated around the room to check that students were using it. Students then copied the school and class rules discussed on the first day of school onto a piece of paper for their notebooks. When they were finished with the seatwork assignment, the teacher discussed a rule that had not been discussed the first day and described course requirements and the grading system.

On the third day of class, Ms. Evans spent about six minutes discussing classroom rules, procedures, and routines with her students. Before the class started she reminded all the students of the beginning routine again. At the end of the class, she reviewed some of the school and class rules and procedures and reminded students that beginning the following day, penalties would be assessed for tardiness, failure to bring materials to class, and other rule violations.

On the fifth day of class, Friday of the first week of school, Ms. Evans devoted abut ten minutes of class time to a discussion and review of procedures and rules. At the beginning of class, she did *not* remind the students about the beginning routine, but she monitored them closely and reminded two students who were slow to start it. Later she assigned a demerit to a student who failed to bring a pen or pencil, reviewing the reason for this procedure and penalty aloud to the class. At the end of the period, she conducted an informal oral "quiz" on class requirements, the grading system, and consequences for some rules and procedures. During the quiz she called on many different students rather than only on students who volunteered. After the quiz she praised the class for how successfully they had completed their first week of school in her class, and she talked with them during the final minutes of the period about their experiences at school during the week.

On the following Monday, the sixth day of school, Ms. Evans closely monitored the beginning class routine and prompted a few students who had forgotten it. She assigned a demerit to a student who failed to bring a pen or pencil. During the class, while students were engaged in a seatwork activity, there was an interruption from an outside visitor. After the visitor had left, the teacher reviewed her expectations for student behavior during interruptions. She also took this opportunity to review several other procedures and rules.

On the tenth day of class, Ms. Evans spent about fifteen minutes carefully explaining procedures that students would be using for a *new* activity: instruction, testing, and seatwork in three spelling groups. She assigned students to groups, explained rationales, and provided specific information about what the activity would involve, what she would be doing during group instruction, and what was expected of the students. She told students when spelling books were to be brought and reviewed the system she had set up for reminding students of materials needed for the next class period.

Monitoring Behavior

An absolutely essential ingredient of management in a low-ability class is monitoring. *You msut be aware of what is occurring in your room.* Keep your eyes on the students and scan the room frequently. If you see inappropriate behavior, deal with it promptly; when possible, use relatively unobtrusive measures to stop it. Simple interventions are best, particularly those that refocus the students' attention on their academic tasks. For example, "If you have questions about this work, raise your hand and I'll come help you." Or "Bill, you should be working on the first five problems, not talking. When you finish number 5, raise your hand and I will check your work." Prompt handling also minimizes the number of students involved and thus avoids creating peer pressure to resist the teacher or show off. Finally, you will give the correct impression of fairness and consistency in handling problems.

Managing Student Work

The cornerstone of an effective accountability system in low-ability classes is an emphasis on daily and weekly grades. Such a system provides students with frequent feedback; it increases students' chances of success by making it difficult for individuals to fall far behind; it allows you to monitor student progress closely; and it helps develop good student work habits. Receiving some kind of grade or credit for effort each day will help students accept responsibility for their schoolwork, especially if you have them keep a record sheet. You will need to allow time in class to show them how to follow this procedure. Have each student compute a weekly grade by calculating an average each week. Of course, you will have to teach them how to do this. Once established as a regular class procedure, it will help your students keep track of their progress. It will also make clear the effects of not completing one or more assignments during the week.

You should also consider making appropriate *participation in class* a part of your grading system. Participation includes answering when called on, volunteering questions, bringing appropriate materials to class, being on time, raising one's hand before speaking, and not calling out to other students or being out of one's seat. Rewarding participation encourages involvement, learning, and attendance. There are several ways to include participation in your grading system. You can give weekly or daily points for each student to add to his or her daily assignment score. You can minimize bookkeeping time by giving participation scores as a closing activity. If your system is simple (for example, 3 points = good participation; 2 points = some; 1 point = a little; 0 = none, or disturbed class), you can award, record in your grade book, and call out points to twenty or so students in two or three minutes at the end of class.

You can also help make students accountable by making it clear that everyone is expected to participate in class discussions. To achieve this use some kind of system that will ensure that you call on every student in turn at least once or twice. You might also keep a weekly answer sheet. Put each student's name on it and give a student a check for acceptable answers during recitation. You can then award points at the end of the week or when figuring weekly averages.

Planning and Presenting Instruction

In low-ability classes more student learning and better classroom behavior are likely to result if (1) you organize classroom instruction into short activity segments with frequent assessments of student understanding, (2) you pay extra attention to presenting directions and instruction clearly, and (3) you build the teaching of study skills into your lessons. When planning classroom activities, avoid activity plans that require students to attend to a presentation or to work continuously for twenty-five or thirty minutes in the same seatwork activity. Instead, use two or more cycles of content development and student seatwork, as described and illustrated in Chapter Seven and in the case study of a mathematics lesson at the end of this chapter. There are two distinct advantages to using several cycles instead of one in lower-ability classes. One advantage is that it is easier to maintain student involvement because of the shorter time segments. Another advantage is that by careful monitoring you can easily observe the extent to which students are able to complete the assignments. This will make it much easier to pace instruction appropriately and to give corrective feedback and repetition during a later content development activity.

When using several instructional cycles, you must be especially aware of two things: pacing and transitions. You'll need to keep track of time in order to leave enough of it for each activity. One way to save enough time for later activities is to plan *brief* student assignments in the first (or the first and second) instructional cycles (for example, a few problems, exercises, questions, and so on) and to do one or two with the students to get them started. Thus, these earlier student assignments become somewhat extended *work samples*. To avoid confusion about the assignment, it is best to write it on the chalkboard or to display it on the overhead projector, even if it is quite short.

If a period contains more than one activity, it will have several transitions. Consequently, efficient transitions are a must. Rely on simple routines and use them very consistently. You might wish to review the discussion of transitions and pacing in Chapter Seven.

Clear communication is important in all classes, but in lower-ability classes clear directions and instruction are especially important; careless, overly complex communication is likely to result in student confusion, frustration, and misbehavior. Follow the guidelines for clarity discussed in Chapter Seven, paying careful attention to the amount of information presented at one time, appropriate vocabulary, and the use of concrete or specific examples to illustrate new concepts. Check for student understanding frequently. Avoid overlapping many procedural directions. Get everyone's attention and then present directions in a step-by-step fashion, waiting for students to complete each step before going on to the next. Finally, as you teach a lower-ability class, be especially aware of opportunities to help your students improve their study and "school survival" skills. For example, assume that you must *teach* all your students how to take notes in your class. Provide demonstration, assistance, practice, monitoring, and feedback. Use content presentations or discussions of the text as vehicles for teaching students how to identify main ideas and supporting evidence. Include in your course some instructional activities that will help students build their vocabularies and improve their computation or memorization skills.

SUGGESTED ACTIVITIES

1.   Chapter Two includes a case study of procedures for small group work in a science class. In addition to procedures for laboratory activities, the case study describes small group discussion procedures that will help you in planning for the use of mixed-ability work groups in your class. Reread this case study.

2.   At the end of this chapter you will find a case study (8-1) of the procedures used by one English teacher for small group instruction in spelling. As you read the case study, think about ways that these procedures might be adapted to your own classroom.

3.   Read case study 8-2, which provides a good illustration of the use of several short content development–student seatwork cycles in a mathematics lesson in a lower-ability class. The case study of an English lesson at the end of Chapter Seven also illustrates instructional procedures that should work well in a lower-ability class.

4.   Three paragraphs at the end of this chapter describe problems frequently faced by teachers of heterogeneous or low-ability classes. After reading each de-

scription, review appropriate parts of this (and other) chapters. Decide what strategies you would recommend to deal with the problems. Discuss each problem scenario with other teachers and make a "brainstorming" list of possible solutions and strategies. Afterward, compare your lists with those included in the keys in Appendix B.

CASE STUDY 8-1:
USING SMALL GROUPS IN ENGLISH

Ms. Hanson uses small group instruction during portions of each class period on two days a week for instruction and testing in spelling. On Tuesdays she meets with each of her three spelling groups for content development and introduction to seatwork on the new words for the week. Students in each group are seated together. This facilitates posting assignments, distributing or collecting papers, and group oral work.

The seatwork assignment for each group is posted near its area of the room. Each group's assignment includes at least one simple introductory task that students can do with no help from the teacher (for example, copying each word five times; looking up words in the dictionary and/or writing sentences with them). After the general instructions are given, all students begin work. The teacher works first with one group, going to its seating area to preview the words, work on pronunciation, and work orally on some of the assignment. She then moves to another group. During the group activity with Ms. Hanson, each student is included in some oral recitation.

At the end of the week, Ms. Hanson uses small groups to administer spelling tests. While students are entering the room, she tells them to get ready for class and instructs them to get out their journals and prepare a sheet of paper for a spelling test. After the bell rings; the teacher introduces two activities which will be proceeding simultaneously: spelling tests for three groups and a composition assignment. She explains the composition (journal) assignment and then reminds the students that she will be going around the room administering spelling tests successively to three spelling groups. When students are not taking the test, they are to work on the journal assignments. Students in each group are seated together. As the students begin work, the teacher begins administering the test to the first spelling group. She stands near the group's desks and uses a low voice. While she gives the test, she also monitors the rest of the class to make sure they remain on task. After she finishes giving the test (about five minutes), the teacher collects the papers, puts them in a specially marked file folder, files them, and goes to the next group. She begins giving the test to the next group but continues to monitor the remainder of the class and signal for quiet when there is some noise from another area.

When the teacher finishes with the second group, she answers questions for students, files the papers, and then goes to the next group and gives the test. While giving the tests, the teacher is careful to monitor the rest of the class, making sure they remain on task. She does not allow students to interrupt her while she is working with another group. When she finishes administering the test to the third spelling group, she collects the spelling papers, files them, and lets the students know how much time they have to finish and proof their composition journal assignment.

CASE STUDY 8-2:
MANAGING INSTRUCTION IN A
LOWER-ABILITY MATH CLASS

Time	Description	Activity
9:25	Mr. Washington begins a lesson on the addition of decimal numbers by describing the purpose of the lesson. He asks review questions on decimals and place value, and he gives several examples using money—dollars and cents. He then puts an addition problem on the chalkboard. The numbers are written on one line (horizontally) and have the same number of place values after the decimal point. He reminds the class that adding decimals is similar to adding whole numbers, but that students must copy the numbers into a column (up and down), being sure that the decimal points are on a straight line (each one above or below the others). They must also be very careful to copy the numbers correctly. He then recopies the problem as column addition, discussing the steps, and tells students to copy the examples. He looks at their work, complimenting them when they copy correctly. He calls on students to perform the addition for the problems and reminds them to be sure to put the decimal in the correct position in the answer. He again uses examples of dollars and cents in order to show the effect of errors and to emphasize the importance of the lesson. Next Mr. Washington puts another example on the board and calls on a student to work it. Edward tries to work through the problem and then says, "Tell me what's wrong!" The teacher says, "Well, let's find out. How can we tell?" The teacher and the class then work through the problem again.	Content Development
9:38	The teacher then displays three new problems on the overhead projector and asks the students to work the problems on the paper they'll be using for the assignment. As the students are working, Mr. Washington circulates, checking to see if the students are doing the problems correctly. He sees one student who has moved the decimal point in some numbers, and he says	Classwork— With Teacher Monitoring and Feedback

CASE STUDY 8-2: (*CONT.*)

Time	Description	Activity
	to the class, "Check to be sure you've copied the problem correctly before you add."	
9:42	After most of the students have completed the problems, the teacher stops them and says, "Let's look up here." He then introduces addition problems having *different* numbers of decimal place values. He works one, explaining how it is similar to and different from the earlier problems. He does two more examples with the class, describing or asking students to describe each step. Mr. Washington then tells students that he is going to do a problem incorrectly and that they should try to catch his mistakes. Afterwards, he and the class do one more example step by step. Then he displays another problem on the overhead projector and directs students to work on it on their papers. Circulating around the room, he sees that all can do it.	Content Development Work Sample
10:00	After discussing the problem, the teacher gives an assignment orally and also writes it on the board. He has the students copy the assignment onto their papers and begin work. As the students work, he walks around, checking on their progress and helping them when necessary. The students work quietly, and the teacher continues to help them throughout the activity.	Seatwork Assignment Monitoring
10:19	One minute before the end of class, Mr. Washington brings the activity to a close, reminds students that the assignment is due tomorrow at the beginning of class, and then makes some general announcements before the bell rings at 10:20. When the bell rings, he dismisses the class.	Closing

Problem A: Heterogeneous Classes

Never before has Ms. Rogers had to deal with students of such different entering achievement levels in her seventh-grade class. She feels frustrated in her efforts to provide instruction at appropriate levels for some students several years below grade level and others above grade level. The brightest students finish seatwork far ahead of the rest of the class, while the slowest students seldom complete an assignment successfully.

So far Ms. Rogers has tried two things. She decided to provide extra-credit activities for students who finish work early, and she has begun to help slower students individually more often during class and after school. Both of these steps seem to help, although each has also created some management problems. What additional things might Ms. Rogers do?

Problem B: Teaching a Low-Ability Class

Sometimes Ms. Porter feels that the students in her low-ability–second-period class are either unwilling or unable to learn anything. Many seem apathetic; they won't even try. Many have short attention spans, and some seem to require constant individual assistance.

At the beginning of the year, Ms. Porter assumed that she would teach her low-ability section much as she would teach the other classes, except for using a slower pace and allowing more practice and drill for the students in the lower-ability section. After several weeks of school, she realized that other adjustments would have to be made as well. She began showing students exactly what to write down for notes during teacher presentations, and she began asking more frequent, simple review questions in class to hold students' attention and help them learn. These measures helped, but many students still don't complete their work successfully. What are some other adjustments Ms. Porter might make in her low-ability section?

Problem C: Student Behavior in a Low-Ability Class

Mr. Oliver is concerned about student behavior in his lower-ability class. Several students are always late coming in. Others frequently forget their books, paper, pencils, assignments, and so on. During content presentations students call out answers or comments; some leave their seats to throw away paper or sharpen their pencils; and there is frequently chatting and note writing. During seatwork assignments students work the first problem or two while teacher is watching but then turn to their neighbors as soon as the teacher turns his back to work with individual students. Mr. Oliver tried to establish order by using a "fine" system; in which students had to write out and turn in definitions or problems if they were caught misbehaving. This system had worked well with his average classes, but in his low-ability class he found he was constantly handing out fines and was unable to keep track of whether they were turned in. What other ideas could Mr. Oliver try?

CHAPTER NINE
EVALUATING
YOUR CLASSROOM'S
ORGANIZATION
AND MANAGEMENT

Effective teachers frequently stop to consider how well their classes are functioning, and then they make changes to improve things when necessary. They are alert about whether class time is being used productively, if students are making satisfactory progress, and whether the class environment is as pleasant and conducive to learning as it should be. If they identify an aspect that could be improved, they are systematic in identifying the source of the problem, seeking solutions, and making changes in their own behavior or in classroom organization. For most teachers, however, evaluating and improving their classroom management and organization is not an easy undertaking. There are several reasons for this. First, many teachers, especially inexperienced ones, are unsure of what *criteria* to use or of what levels of management success to expect. After all, no class of secondary students is completely cooperative and task oriented, and no teacher is totally organized, efficient, and clear at all times. Furthermore, teachers seldom have the opportunity to observe in other teachers' classrooms, so they may have a limited perspective from which to view their own situation. Finally, it is difficult both to teach and to observe one's own classes systematically without a very clear idea of what management indicators are important.

This chapter is designed to help you as you evaluate or make plans to improve your own management effectiveness. First, some major indicators of management effectiveness are identified and levels of acceptable or expected class performance are suggested for each. Next, to help you in diagnosing the causes of a problem, we have provided a series of questions relating to each of six areas that are often the basis for management problems. Because the areas and questions are keyed to the chapters in this book, the chapter will also serve as a basis for applying and reviewing key concepts and principles that have been emphasized. Problem vignettes presented at the end of the chapter will allow you to test your skills at diagnosing management difficulties and identifying alternate courses of action.

DETERMINING WHEN CHANGES ARE NEEDED

To decide whether or where there might be room for improvement in the management or organization of your classroom, we suggest that you consider the effects of your management system on the behavior of your students. Using student behavior as a criterion for management effectiveness is reasonable because one of the main goals of classroom management is to foster student cooperation and involvement in learning activities. Also, student behaviors provide management indicators that are relatively easy to observe. For example, major signs of management problems include frequent failure by many students to complete assignments satisfactorily, high rates of off-task behavior, widespread lack of cooperation, and frequent disruption of classroom activities. Levels of acceptable or desirable class behavior on each of these indicators are difficult to state with certainty because of differing school practices, varying tolerance levels of teachers and students, and divergent expectations for behavior for different activities, groups of students, and age/grade levels. We will, however, provide approximate guidelines for levels of these indicators that are often seen in well-managed classrooms. These estimates are based on observations from our own research as well as data from other studies using measures of student behavior.

On-task Rates

This indicator is defined as the number of students who are appropriately engaged in whatever classroom activity is occurring. Being on task does not necessarily mean that a student is highly involved or participating enthusiastically, but it does mean that no obvious sign of inattention or inappropriate behavior is apparent and that the student is doing whatever the situation calls for. In teacher-led–whole-class activities, a well-managed class typically will have around 90 percent or higher on-task rates. Thus, in a class of twenty-five to thirty students, no more than two or three students on the average would be off task at any given time in such activities. Off-task students would generally *not* be engaged in disruptive behavior, but they might be momentarily socializing, out of their seats, daydreaming, or simply not working. We would not usually expect any individual student to remain off task for very long, and certainly not throughout an entire activity.

Disruptive Behavior

Student behavior is disruptive when it seriously interferes with the activities of the teacher or of several students for more than a brief time. Examples of such behavior include continuously bothering neighboring students, creating confusion or making loud noises during a lesson, excessive attention seeking, acting out, and hostile, aggressive responses to other students or to the teacher. Disruptive behavior varies in intensity from relatively mild forms to very severe types. In well-managed classes disruptive behaviors are not common and are usually limited to mild and brief incidents, generally occurring no more than once per hour. When a more severe disturbance occurs, it is almost always an isolated incident, and the teacher takes immediate action to deal with it.

Student Cooperation

Well-managed classrooms usually are pleasant environments for students and the teacher. Students should not, after the first several weeks of classes, need constant reminders to follow rules and procedures, and they should follow the teacher's directions without excessive delay or complaints. They should be tolerant of each others' needs and willing to abide by group decisions and work within the class routines that you have established. A problem in this area is indicated when many students continue to test limits, disregard class rules and major procedures, and display rudeness and intolerance toward each other or toward the teacher.

Completion of Assignments

Although failure to complete assignments suggests instructional, motivational, or learning difficulties, it can also be an indicator of management problems. *Frequent* failure to complete assignments means that more than one or two students often do not complete their work on time. This may involve the same students or different students. Of course, frequent failure by any student should be of concern and should receive your attention. However, it is only when *several* students frequently fail to complete assignments that a management problem is suggested. Although classroom management variables are not likely to be the sole causes, changes in accountability procedures, in rewards, or in the way instruction is organized and presented can help alleviate the problem.

If levels of on-task behavior, disruption, cooperation, and assignment completion in your classroom are very different from the levels in the well-managed classes described in the preceding paragraphs, adjustments in your management system may be called for. Some allowances should be made, however, for student behavior in very large classes as well as in classes with many low-achieving students or with a high proportion of boys. Such classes will often have more off-task or inappropriate behavior. Thus, in such classes you might have one or two more off-task students, on the average, and perhaps a bit more frequent disruptive behavior before you need worry that management problems may be developing. Also, you should not overreact to an occasional bad day or lesson. The day before a holiday and the last period of the day will often be more difficult times to maintain student involvement. The key question is: Are one or more management indicators at undesirable levels on a regular basis? If so, then you should evaluate your management plan and try to improve it. Note that the presence of a problem does not mean that a class is *poorly* managed. A teacher can have good management skills but still have some room for improvement. It may also be the case that solving a particular management problem may change an average situation into an excellent one. However, even classrooms having widespread management problems can be improved. The time and effort required will pay off eventually with better student behavior and a classroom setting more conducive to learning.

You may wish to gather more evidence before proceeding. One possibility is to keep a log of class behavior for a week. Write a short daily summary of the events and behavior during activities that seem to have problems. This record will allow you to decide whether problems are recurrent and not just the result of unusual circumstances. The process of keeping a record may also help you identify what is *causing* the difficulties. Another possibility for gathering evidence is to ask a colleague to observe you teach. While the opportunity to observe fellow teachers is limited, someone might be able to observe you during his or her preparation and planning period. One other option is to ask an administrator, supervisor, or special teacher whose schedule may be more flexible to observe you. Needless to say, such a person must be one whose opinion you trust and who will be helpful rather than threatening to you. Before the observation talk with your observer about your areas of concern and about what kind of feedback you would like to receive.

DIAGNOSING THE CAUSE OF A PROBLEM

Once a problem is recognized, the next step is to identify what is causing it. Self-diagnosis is always an uncertain art, so if possible, the advice of others should be sought, preferably from those who have observed you in your class. In addition, the questions in the six areas presented below will help pinpoint sources of management problems. This self-evaluation guide is keyed to relevant chapters of this book. It is organized into six management areas, with specific indicators to help identify sources of possible problems in each area. Even if you are not experiencing management problems to any great degree, you may find it helpful to review the guide, because you may discover an item or two that you could modify to good effect.

Reevaluate Your Room Arrangement

Ask yourself the following questions to determine if your classroom space and materials are well organized.

Does congestion frequently occur in certain areas of the room, such as at the pencil sharpener, materials center, or at your desk?

Can you and your students move around the room easily, or are traffic lanes blocked by desks or other furniture or equipment?

Can you see all students from any place in the room at which you instruct or work?

During your presentations can students see the overhead projector screen and the main chalkboard areas without turning around or moving from their chairs or desks?

Are students who frequently need your attention or assistance seated where you can easily monitor and reach them?

Do some students frequently bother others who sit near them?

If the answer to one or more of the above questions is yes, then some aspects of your room arrangement could be at fault, and a change may be in order. If the problem is obvious and easily corrected, such as a change of seats for a few students who are distracting each other, make the change without delay. If the problem is more complicated, use the material presented in Chapter One as a guide for comprehensive review of your present room arrangement.

Note that some of the problems implied by the above questions could have other contributing causes. For example, if students are distracting each other, the problem might be caused by poor monitoring, inadequate consequences, or excessively long periods of seatwork rather than by the seating arrangement. Thus, consider your ideas about the causes of a problem as hypotheses that may or may not explain the entire situation. Don't let an initial insight blind you to other possibilities.

Review Your Rules and Procedures for Student Conduct

Have you stopped enforcing one or more of your rules?

Are your major class procedures (that is, governing things such as student talk, raising hands, moving around the room, use of equipment and supplies) being followed without constant prompting and reminders?

Are some student behaviors occurring that are clearly undesirable but which are not covered under your current rules or procedures?

Do you find yourself giving the same directions repeatedly for some common procedure?

Are you spending as much time going over directions and procedures now as at the beginning of the year?

Affirmative answers to these questions indicate potential problems in some procedural area. You will find it worthwhile to review Checklist 2 and the descriptions of commonly used procedures in Chapter Two. If you decide to modify an existing rule or procedure or to install a new one, do so as carefully as if it were the beginning of the year. Explain the change or new procedure clearly, demonstrate it if necessary, watch students as they follow the new procedure, and give them corrective or supportive feedback as appropriate.

The fact that a rule or procedure is not working does not necessarily mean that it is inappropriate and should be changed. Instead, it may mean that the procedure or rule needs better consequences or more careful monitoring. Thus, before you change a major procedure, be sure to consider whether other aspects of your management system need a tune up. In particular, you should review the material in Chapter Four on rewards and penalties.

Review Your Procedures for Managing Student Work

Do many of your students fail to complete assignments or not turn them in at all?

Is much student work messy to the point of being illegible?

Are students completing work on time, or do you find yourself giving extensions more and more frequently?

Do students sometimes claim they didn't know an assignment was due or what its requirements were?

After grades are given on report cards, do students frequently complain that they do not understand why they received particular grades?

These questions indicate potential problems with accountability procedures, including grading, other feedback procedures, monitoring student work in progress, and communicating assignments and work requirements. Of course, other reasons for failure to complete assignments should be considered, including a mismatch between task demands and student capability, or incomplete understanding of the content. However, a review of the material in Chapter Three should provide some additional help in establishing better levels of student responsibility for their work.

List the Consequences for Appropriate and Inappropriate Behavior, and Review How Frequently They Are Used and How Effective They Are

Do you reward good student behavior, including effort, in a variety of ways?

Are your rewards still attractive to students, or have students tired of them?

Do you find yourself assessing penalties more and more often and rewarding students less than you did previously?

Are you warning and threatening students frequently, and do you fail to follow through when students continue to misbehave?

Have your penalties lost their deterrent value through overuse?

Does administering your reward or penalty system take too much time and effort?

You should consider varying or adding to your rewards occasionally, when they seem to be losing their appeal. Also, limited but consistent use of penalties is necessary in order for them to retain their effectiveness. Review the recommendations in Chapter Four for some ideas and examples of consequence systems. Also, check Chapter Six for some simple strategies that do not involve the use of penalties for dealing with inappropriate behavior.

Consider Whether You are Detecting Misbehavior in its Early Stages and Preventing Little Problems from Developing into Big Ones

Do you tend to notice misbehavior only after it involves several students?

When you work with students in groups or individually at your desk, does noise, disruption, or widespread work avoidance occur?

Do you sometimes have the feeling that some students are misbehaving simply to gain your attention?

Are there times when so much inappropriate behavior occurs at once that you don't have any idea what to do?

Do you sometimes discover that students have hardly begun classwork assignments when they should actually be through with them?

If you are experiencing problems in this area, you need to work on your skills for monitoring and dealing promptly with inappropriate behavior. Sometimes teachers who have difficulty catching misbehavior early tend to become overly absorbed in their immediate situation and lose sight (literally) of the whole classroom setting. Such tunnel vision causes them to overlook incipient problems at the periphery of the class. Small problems are likely to become big ones when teachers ignore too much inappropriate behavior, fail to use simple, unobtrusive strategies to help students get back on task, or overreact to relatively minor events, giving them inappropriate attention. Suggestions for monitoring and responding to inappropriate behavior can be found in Chapter Six.

Consider Ways to Improve the Management of Your Instructional Activities

Do students frequently seem confused about work requirements, and do they fail to follow directions, even after you have explained them or listed them on the board?

Do you often discover that students have not understood your presentations and that they therefore cannot complete assignments correctly?

When students are frequently confused and unable to follow directions, you should suspect problems with the clarity of presentations. Being clear involves more than just repeating information or instructions, so give careful consideration to the tips in Chapter Seven on teaching clearly.

Are transitions from one activity to another taking a long time?
Are some students not ready for instruction when a new activity begins?
Is there widespread misbehavior during transitions?

Transition points can be a source of distress if they are not handled carefully. Ideas for structuring transitions are presented in Chapter Seven along with the material on activity management and clarity.

Do you have students with learning problems who seem to require more assistance than you are giving them?
Is there a constant demand for free-time materials and activities in your class?
Is the performance of many of your students well below grade level in basic skills areas?
Are some of your students so fast at finishing classwork that they get bored or bother others?
Do you find that only a relatively small group of students monopolizes class discussions?
Are a few of your students so far behind the class that you have virtually given up on them?

Ideas for managing classes with students working well below grade level or with a very wide ability range are presented in Chapter Eight. Good management in such classes is especially important because of the need to provide extra assistance and supervision for certain students.

IMPLEMENTING CHANGES IN YOUR CLASSROOM

If you decide that some change in your classroom management system is required, then you'll need to plan when and how to do it. Some changes will be simple to plan and carry out; others will be more complex.

Less Complex Changes

The least complicated changes are those that involve only your own behavior. For example, you may decide that you need to review or reteach certain procedures, be more consistent in your enforcement of certain rules, or monitor student behavior and work more carefully. Such changes can be undertaken at once and require only your own resolve and self-monitoring to carry them out. However, succeeding in such a change may not be as easy as attempting it; like New Year's resolutions, attempts to alter established behavior patterns are sometimes short-lived. Help yourself make such changes by *writing down* a plan that specifies exactly what you intend to do. For example, if you decide you are going to try to monitor student behavior more carefully, you might note the following:

> During whole-class presentations I will observe the class, looking at each student, at least twice a minute.
>
> During seatwork I will check each student's progress during the first few minutes of the activity and at least one other time, and check the work of students who have problems completing assignments several other times.

At the beginning of each day, read over your plan. Try to follow it consistently during your classes. Then review the plan at the end of each day to evaluate your progress and to make necessary alterations or additions. Besides committing yourself to a change, writing it out in detail will help make it more specific and concrete and therefore more likely to be implemented. If you find that you forget to carry out the plan, try writing notes to yourself, and then put them in places that will remind you at appropriate times. For example, make notes on 3" × 5" cards— "Remember to monitor"—and clip one to your lesson plan book and to the teachers' edition of your textbooks.

Other less complicated changes to make are alterations in seating assignments, room arrangement, the schedule of activities, and procedures that regulate student behaviors that occur infrequently. For such changes you may simply define the expected behavior or change, describe or discuss a rationale with the students, and then monitor student compliance.

More Complex Changes

Any change that requires students to alter behavior that occurs frequently will be more complex than one that entails only a change by the teacher or a minor change by students. Not only are old habits hard to break, but because the behavior occurs frequently, more opportunities will exist for students to avoid the new behaviors. An example of a more complex change is requiring that students raise their hands and wait to be called on after they have become accustomed to calling out without raising hands. Another more complex and difficult change is obtaining completed work from students who have become habitual work avoiders.

To bring about complex changes, several steps are necessary. The desired change and reasons for it should first be discussed with the students. This discussion should include obtaining a commitment from the students to make the change. The discussion should also include an identification of any new consequences for appropriate or inappropriate behavior. Then, once the instructions have been given, the teacher must monitor initial trials carefully, provide corrective feedback, encouragement, and rewards, as needed, and remain alert to proper implementation until the new behavior has taken hold.

When Should Changes be Made?

Simple changes can be made at almost any time. They should not, however, be capricious. Before making a simple change (for example, in room arrangement, grading procedures, procedures regulating infrequent student behavior), review other related aspects of your management system to be sure that you are altering the correct component—then make the change whenever it appears appropriate.

More complex changes require careful planning. The greatest danger is that you might try a change before you are ready for it. Once you have diagnosed a problem, it will be natural to want to make immediate corrective action. However, if the change is not properly planned, it is less likely to succeed. Therefore, be sure to make major changes only after you have carefully considered alternatives. Be sure you know exactly what behaviors will be expected of students and that you have enough time to explain and to monitor the change. Then, once your planning is complete, you are ready to initiate the new behavior.

Good times to review your management plans and to make changes, especially major ones, are the start of a new grading period or the day immediately after a vacation break. Classes are usually more attentive and cooperative at such times, and they will be more accepting of change. Some classes may need a review of class rules and procedures anyway, so this is a natural time to introduce a change. In fact, you can enlist the students' help in making changes by noting that they are starting a new grading period or beginning over after a vacation, so this is a chance to make a fresh start.

SUGGESTED ACTIVITIES

Three case studies of classes with management problems are presented below. After reading each one, try to identify the major problem areas and then describe what each teacher could do to manage these classes more effectively. After you have completed each case study, compare your suggestions to the answer key in Appendix B. These case studies will also be good for small group discussions; individuals will bring different perspectives to each case, and different solutions may be offered.

CASE STUDY 9-1:
CONDUCT PROBLEMS IN A HISTORY CLASS

When the school year began, Mr. Davis told his American History classes that he had just one major rule for conduct—the Golden Rule. "If you'll treat others as you want to be treated, then we'll get along fine," he said. Then he added, "Just be sure to respect each others' rights, and that includes mine, and we'll all have a good year." Mr. Davis also told his students that he expected them to behave maturely, because they were in high school, and that if one of them got out of line, he would be quite willing to send that student to the school office to be dealt with by the assistant principal.

The classes did, indeed, function without major disruptions for several weeks. Gradually however, almost imperceptibly, Mr. Davis began having difficulty getting students settled down to start the daily lesson. And once begun, presentations to the class and class discussions seemed to be conducted with an undercurrent of noise, as students whispered, joked, and socialized. Mr. Davis found himself interrupting the lessons more and more often to call for quiet or to remind students of what they were supposed to be doing. Problems were occurring in each class period but were worst in the sixth, the last period of the day. By the end of the fourth week of classes, Mr. Davis had sent two students to the office for persistent talking during class, including talking back to him when he asked them to be quiet. Sixth-period behavior was better for a day or so afterward, but students were soon back to being noisy and inattentive. The following description of the sixth-period class a few days later is typical.

At the beginning of the period, Mr. Davis had written a discussion question on the chalkboard. While Mr. Davis checked roll and returned papers, students were supposed to write a paragraph answering the question in preparation for a class discussion. However, only about half the class actually did the work; other students talked, several sat doing nothing, and two students were out of their seats socializing. Mr. Davis asked one student to sit down, but he didn't. When he told a particularly noisy girl to "close your mouth," she responded, "I can't." During the discussion students who were talking at the beginning of class complained that they did not understand the question. A few students raised their hands to volunteer responses during the discussion, and Mr. Davis called on them; other students called out responses, sometimes silly ones. Later Mr. Davis assigned questions for the end of the chapter to be turned in the next day. Most students worked on this assignment in class, although some read magazines or talked instead. Three students passed magazines back and forth until Mr. Davis told them to put the magazines away. The noise level built up and ten minutes before the end of the period, most students had stopped working and were conversing.

What are some things Mr. Davis might do to establish better behavior in his classes?

CASE STUDY 9-2:
POOR WORK AND STUDY HABITS IN MATHEMATICS

Ms. Woods's mathematics classes are free of serious disruptions, and for the most part, students pay attention to her presentations. In her first-year and second-year algebra classes, in which most of the students are very conscious of report card grades and seem serious about doing well in school, conduct problems are limited to isolated cases. In the three sections of general mathematics that Ms. Woods teaches, students are less task oriented and more inclined to misbehave. Nonetheless, students usually observe major class rules and procedures, with most of the inappropriate behavior being limited to off-task socializing or inattentiveness.

Ms. Woods's classes are not without problems, however; numerous students are falling behind in their work and are receiving low grades as a result of their poor performance on chapter tests. These tests are used as 75 percent of the report card grade, with the remaining 25 percent based on a score assigned to each student's notebook, which is turned in at the end of the grading period. At the beginning of the year, students were told to keep all classwork and homework assignments in the notebook along with any daily notes they might take. Their notebook grade is based on an overall score assigned by the teacher one week before the end of the grading period. "After you check each assignment in class, be certain to place it in the notebook so that it will be there when I determine notebook grades," Ms. Woods told her students. "Otherwise, you will not receive credit for doing your assignments." About once a week Ms. Woods collects daily work and checks it herself; however, numerous students do not turn in completed homework assignments. The students in the algebra classes have followed the instructions for notebooks reasonably well, although several in each class have presented incomplete notebooks at grading time. In the general math classes, more of the student notebooks are poorly done, with many assignments missing and contents sloppily assembled. A handful of students in each class have not bothered to turn in notebooks at all. Ms. Woods found herself getting annoyed a few days before the notebooks were due, when many students asked what was supposed to be in them. As a result of the confusion over the contents, Ms. Woods allowed an extra several days for students to turn in the notebooks, and she told students to listen more carefully the next time she explained a course requirement.

During presentations to classes Ms. Woods holds students' attention well because she presents new concepts and procedures clearly. She always explains each type of problem that students are likely to encounter, and she demonstrates solutions and a rationale using several examples. Ms. Woods generally works at her desk while students do seatwork, although she allows them to come up to her desk for assistance when they encounter difficulty or when they need to determine what work they have missed while they were absent. As the year has progressed, Ms. Woods has observed more and more students doing poor work on their exams, presenting incomplete or sloppy notebooks, and receiving low grades. What could she do to improve student performance and work completion?

CASE STUDY 9-3:
A SCIENCE LESSON

The following case study is a description of a general science lesson conducted during the second week of school. What problems are evident, and what changes would be appropriate?

After checking roll Ms. Grant tells students that the day's activity will be their first lab assignment and that they will work in groups. "The purpose of the lab work is to get practice with the scientific method," she says, and she lists the stages: observation, formulation of hypothesis, gathering evidence, analysis, and conclusions. Ms. Grant tells students that they must work together in an assigned lab group, and she calls out the group assignments, forming six groups of four or five students each. Students are then told to arrange their desks according to groups. Students are very noisy as they do so, with much playing and talking occurring. Ms. Grant has to speak very loudly in order to regain the students' attention and to give directions for a dittoed lab sheet that she distributes to each student. Standing at the front of the room, the teacher reads the directions on the lab sheet while several students continue to converse throughout the instructions. Two groups at the back of the room do not pay attention to the teacher's presentation of directions. Ms. Grant tells students that each group will get a box with something inside and that they should try to determine what it is. They must work together with their partners in the group on the task. Having said that, Ms. Grant distributes to each group a small box, wrapped in construction paper. Students immediately treat the boxes as noise makers, causing more commotion. Ms. Grant yells above the din, "Be sure to fill in three guesses at the bottom of the dittoed page."

During the ensuing activity only one group discusses what possibilities exist and how they might determine what the box contains. The other groups mainly record the first three guesses that are offered by group members. The teacher observes the groups from a stool at the front of the room. After four minutes she says, "List the tests that you performed. Then put down your three best guesses." After six minutes four of the groups are finished, and students put the boxes back on the teacher's desk. Two groups continue to work on the problem, while the remaining students sit idle or talk. One boy calls out, "When are we going to start?" The teacher responds, "Soon, when everyone is ready." After two more minutes the teacher says, "Listen up, we are ready for the group reports." Some students are still talking while Ms. Grant gives directions for each group's oral report. One student from each group will give the group report, which is to be a statement of each guess and the reasons for it. The teacher also reminds students to follow class rules for listening when other students talk and for not leaving their seats during discussions. "If you can't keep your mouth shut, we won't be able to do activities like this," she notes. While giving reports, students speak softly; it is difficult to hear each report because of talking and fooling around by a number of students. The students' reports are short, and the teacher's comments are limited to brief evaluations and indications of acceptance, such as, "Okay," "Good," or "Good observation." Ms. Grant does not record nor compare group observations or guesses, but she occasionally asks for clarification, such as, "What makes you guess that?" After about ten minutes each group report has been given, although many students have not paid attention to any report except the one from their own group. Ms. Grant tells students, "You used a lot of good observations, like the last group that distinguished between round objects and objects with flat sides. Most of the groups were close, and tomorrow I'll tell you what was in each box. Please pass your papers in." After papers have been collected, Ms. Grant asks two students to distribute a classroom set of books. She tells the class to begin reading a chapter on molecules for the next day. After several minutes of commotion, students settle down and read silently for the remaining thirteen minutes of class.

What problems are evident and what changes would be appropriate?

APPENDIX A
FURTHER READINGS
ON CLASSROOM
MANAGEMENT
AND DISCIPLINE

Association for Supervision and Curriculum Development. *Effective Classroom Management for the Elementary School* (Videotape). Alexandria, Va: Associaton for Supervision and Curriculum Development, 1981. This half-hour videotape shows excerpts from the first day of school in a very effective teacher's classroom. Many concepts presented in this book are illustrated.

Canter, L., and Canter, M. *Assertive Discipline.* Los Angeles, Calif.: Canter and Associates, 1976. The Canters stress that teachers must assert their right to teach in an orderly and disruption-free environment. To accomplish this, teachers must establish rules governing classroom conduct and enforce these rules with a set of clearly defined consequences. A variety of supplementary materials, including videotapes and filmstrips are also available.

Clarizio, H. F. *Toward Positive Classroom Discipline* (2nd ed.). New York: John Wiley, 1976. This book presents many applications of the behavioral or learning theory approach to classroom discipline. Much of the book (and the behavior modification literature generally) is focused on techniques for dealing with disruptive behavior and developing more appropriate behaviors. Because of its extensive treatment of reward and punishment, this book is especially appropriate as a supplement to Chapter Four (Rewards and Penalties) and Chapter Six (Maintaining Good Behavior) in our text.

Doyle, W. *Classroom Management.* West Lafayette, Ind.: Kappa Delta Phi, P.O. Box A, 1980. This 31-page booklet is a concise and readable summary of major concepts needed to understand the teacher's classroom management tasks. Defining the teacher's immediate task as "to gain and maintain the cooperation of the students in activities that fill classroom time," Doyle examines a variety of factors that influence what teachers do, and he also describes teacher behaviors that contribute to effective management.

Dreikurs, R., Grunwald, B., and Pepper, F. *Maintaining Sanity in the Classroom: Classroom Management Techniques* (2nd ed.). New York: Harper and Row, 1982. Dreikurs regards misbehavior as deriving from mistaken goals: seeking attention, power, revenge, or withdrawal. Only when the individual perceives a connection between behavior and its logical and natural consequences will appropriate change take place. Thus, planning the classroom environment so that the students understand the consequences of their behavior is essential to promoting effective discipline. The book contains many suggestions and applications for teachers.

Duke, D., ed. *Classroom Management. The 78th Yearbook of the National Society of Education, Part II.* Chicago: University of Chicago Press, 1979.

Duke, D., ed. *Helping Teachers Manage Classrooms.* Alexandria, Va.: Association for Supervision and Curriculum Development, 1982. The two books edited by Duke are collections of articles reviewing different aspects of classroom management. Some of the chapters summarize research, while others consider more theoretical or conceptual issues. These books will give the reader a thorough overview of the field and will provide many helpful references for following up particular lines of inquiry.

Gazda, G., et al. *Human Relations Development: A Manual for Educators* (2nd ed.). Boston: Allyn and Bacon, 1977. This book emphasizes the teacher's skills in developing interpersonal communication and relationships. Because teachers interact daily with many children or adolescents, as well as with parents and other adults, they must be able to listen and respond in ways that facilitate understanding, avoid miscommunication, and solve problems. The book contains many exercises to aid the reader in developing such skills.

Glasser, W., et al. *The Reality Therapy Reader: A Survey of the Work of William Glasser.* New York: Harper and Row, 1976. Reality therapy is an approach to dealing with individuals that attempts to get them to choose more appropriate behavior. Widely used in school settings, this approach involves clearly identifying consequences for student behavior and being sure that the student understands them. Reality therapy probably works best when it is adopted as a schoolwide system of discipline; however, there is much valuable information for the individual teacher who must deal with inappropriate behavior.

Good, T. L., and Brophy, J. *Looking in Classrooms* (2nd ed.). New York: Harper and Row, 1978. Two good chapters on classroom management in this book make it a valuable source for teachers looking for a readable summary of classroom management applications. Other chapters treat topics related to classroom management, such as teacher expectations, modeling, and grouping.

Gordon, T. *Teacher Effectiveness Training.* New York: Peter H. Wyden, 1974. This book emphasizes the teacher's ability to communicate effectively with students. Listening skills and techniques for dealing constructively with students when their misbehavior causes a problem are described. Although Gordon's approach is not a comprehensive management program, it does offer skills that are helpful for talking with students about their behavior.

Kounin, J. *Discipline and Group Management in Classrooms.* New York: Holt, Rinehart and Winston, 1970. This book reports the results of several of Kounin's studies of group management. Along with behavior modification research, it forms the basis for much current thinking about effective management. This book was not intended to be a compendium of suggestions for classroom teachers, but it does provide informative and clear illustrations of key teacher behaviors.

Readers interested in other publications on classroom management by this book's authors can select from the following references.

Clements, B. S., and Evertson, C. M. "Orchestrating Small Group Instruction in Elementary School Classrooms." Austin, Texas: The Research and Development Center for Teacher Education, 1982, Report No. 6053, 34pp.

Emmer, E. T., and Evertson, C. M. "Synthesis of Research on Classroom Management." *Educational Leadership*, 1981, *38*, 342–347.

Emmer, E. T., Evertson, C. M., and Anderson, L. M. "Effective Classroom Management at the Beginning of the School Year." *The Elementary School Journal*, 1980, *80*, 219–231.

Evertson, C. M., and Emmer, E. T. "Effective Management at the Beginning of the School Year in Junior High Classes." *Journal of Educational Psychology*, 1982, *74*, 485–498.

Evertson, C. M. "Differences in Instructional Activities in Higher- and Lower-Achieving Junior High English and Math Classes." *The Elementary School Journal*, 1982, *82*, 329–350.

Evertson, C. M., Emmer, E. T., Clements, B. S., Sanford, J. P., and Worsham, M. E. *Classroom Management for Elementary Teachers.* Englewood Cliffs, N. J.: Prentice-Hall, Inc., 1984.

Evertson, C. M., Sanford, J. P., and Emmer, E. T. "Effects of Class Heterogeneity in Junior High School." *American Educational Research Journal*, 1981, *18*, 219–232.

Sanford, J. P., Emmer, E. T., and Clements, B. S. "Improving Classroom Management." *Educational Leadership*, 1983, *40*, 56–61.

APPENDIX B
ANSWER KEYS
FOR CHAPTER ACTIVITIES

CHAPTER ONE

The room arrangement shown in Figure 1-2 will contribute to classroom management problems in a number of ways. Specific items are listed below.

Students at the rear of the row furthest left will have difficulty seeing the overhead projector screen.

When the teacher stands at the overhead projector, six students will be seated behind her.

Desks are arranged so that students face other students. Although this formation may be useful during class discussions for encouraging students to respond to each other, it may produce a high level of distraction during other activities.

Some student desks face windows, which might also be a source of distraction. These same desks face away from a chalkboard.

The group of four desks on the right-hand side of the room is in front of the bookshelf and impedes movement in that area of the room. Students at those desks are likely to be distracted by students using materials or equipment at that end of the room.

The wastebasket is not conveniently located; a place nearer the door would be better.

The table is too near the teacher's desk and crowds several student desks. Students working at the table might disturb others nearby. Traffic flow in the area around the teacher's desk and table is poor.

The major instructional area by the overhead projector has no table, desk, or other storage space to hold materials needed in presentations.

Chapter Six
Problem A

Ms. Marcus should review her expectations for student behavior in the problem areas to be sure they are clear, reasonable, and concretely stated. At the beginning of class the next day, she should discuss them with the students. The following suggestions might also help improve behavior.

Circulate among the students and monitor the class continuously in order to anticipate and prevent misbehavior before it occurs.

Make sure the students have enough work to do, that they understand the assignment, and that they know what to do after they finish it. Circulate and look at all the students' papers to be sure they are following directions and are able to do the work.

Whenever possible, statements about behavior should be work related and positively stated:

"You should be working on problems 6 through 15, and they should be done silently."

After you have turned in your assignment, you may read your library book or work on an assignment from another class."

"If you are having problems with this assignment, raise your hand and I'll come to your desk."

Decide what minor inappropriate student behavior can be ignored so that lessons are not constantly interrupted to deal with behavior that is unlikely to persist or cause a problem.

Be sure that stated consequences are appropriate to the behavior and that they are carried out consistently. Positive consequences for appropriate behavior should also be included in the list of specific consequences.

No more than one warning should be given before following through with consequences.

Problem B

Ms. Jones could use the following strategies to deal with these students.

Greg

Check Greg's academic record or talk to Greg's other teachers to find out if his behavior is typical. If not, then call Greg's parents or arrange a conference with Greg to get at the reasons for his poor participation.

If Greg's behavior is typical, and if he has limited ability in the subject, he can be seated next to the presentation area where he can be monitored easily. Check with him after giving directions to be sure he understands the assignment. Then stand by him to be sure he gets started on his work.

Check with Greg frequently throughout the period to see if he is working on the assignment and to provide necessary help.

Whenever possible, break up the assignments into parts or reduce the assignments for Greg to prevent the possibility of his feeling overwhelmed. Have him show two or three answers after five minutes, two or three after the next five minutes, and so on. These checks should be initiated by the teacher until Greg assumes responsibility. As the year progresses, the amount of work required and the length of time between checks can be increased gradually. Offer a bonus of five minutes free time at the end of the period of Greg completes his required work.

Joe

Avoid overreacting to Joe's attempts to get attention. Make clear to him what behavior is acceptable and have Joe formulate a plan for developing more appropriate behavior.

Identify some constructive things Joe can do that would provide recognition (for example, preparing an oral report for extra credit, raising his hand and waiting to be called on before responding).

Set specific consequences for his turning around, speaking out without permission, and making inappropriate comments; then follow through consistently in carrying these out. Consequences for breaking the rules may include things such as having to wait in his seat one minute after the class leaves for the next period, sitting in the hall to do his work, or receiving detention or being sent to the school office after receiving a certain number of demerits.

If Joe's behavior does not improve, he can be required to write a contract in which he agrees to practice appropriate behavior and stop particular misbehaviors. Joe's parents should also be called to discuss his behavior and to get suggestions for working with him.

If Joe continues to be uncooperative, he can be seated away from other students with his face to a wall, out in the hallway, or behind a screen. The next day, if his behavior has improved, a system can be tried in which he can earn his way back into the class with a full period of appropriate behavior. He should be allowed to remain with the class only as long as his behavior is in compliance with the classroom rules.

Chapter Seven
Problem A

The following suggestions for Ms. Carpenter would help improve her student' comprehension.

Outline the lesson sequence, breaking down complex lessons into smaller, easier-to-understand parts or steps. Be sure to define words that students may not know.

During presentations let students know what they are expected to write in their notes by underlining important points as they are written on the chalkboard, or by displaying them on an overhead projector transparency. Another way to structure note taking is to give students an outline with space for additional notes.

During content development activities obtain frequent work samples by having students do problems or answer questions. Circulate during these times, checking for areas of confusion, common problems, and students who are not participating. Based on feedback from these samples, adjust instruction either by slowing down or by increasing the pace of the presentation, or by repeating content where necessary.

Be sure students know the purpose of the lesson, and at the end of presentations, always restate major objectives or else quiz students on important points.

Give students step-by-step instructions for assignments. Check to be sure they understand what they are to do, and then help them pace their work by telling them how long the assignment should take to complete and warning them when there is a short time left.

Circulate while students are doing seatwork assignments. Check to be sure they are working on the assignment, that they are doing it correctly, and that they are using their time wisely.

If it becomes apparent during a seatwork or recitation activity that some students do not understand the material, have them join you in a small group after the general presentation. At this time you can review the points of the lesson and answer questions.

Problem B

Mr. Miller could reduce the amount of time wasted by his class if he would use the following approaches.

Use an academic warm-up as part of the beginning-of-class routine. Have the warm-up written on the chalkboard or displayed on an overhead transparency, and require that students complete the task in a set period of time (for example, five minutes). Be sure that warm-up activities are checked and that they count toward the students' grades.

Use established routines as much as possible for beginning and ending lessons, passing and collecting papers and supplies, and exchanging papers to grade. Monitor to be sure students follow routines.

Teach students exactly what behaviors are expected during transitions: voice level, pencil sharpener use, procedures for passing papers, and so on.

Give instructions for what is to be done *before* beginning transitions, not during them.

Post assignments where all students can see them. Begin seatwork assignments together as a class, doing the first problems or answering the first question as a group. Then monitor at the beginning of seatwork to be sure everyone gets off to a good start.

Chapter Eight
Problem A

To deal with very diverse ability levels, Ms. Rogers might try the following approaches.

If one or two students are especially likely to have trouble with whole-class assignments, these students can be seated where the teacher can easily keep an eye on them during instruction and seatwork. As soon as seatwork instructions have been given to the whole class and the teacher has monitored to be sure they have begun work, she can check with slower students privately to go over instructions again or to modify the assignment, as necessary. These instructions and directions can be done as a small group activity if more than one or two students need the extra assistance.

Enrichment or extra-credit material for students who finish classwork early should include work-related activities that will not distract other students. Feedback, credit, and recognition for completion of enrichment activities should be a part of the system.

All students in the class should be involved in discussion or recitation sessions. Systematically calling on each student will give everyone an opportunity to participate.

If the above suggestions are not sufficient for a given class, small group instruction might be used for part of the course work. Procedures for group work must be planned, then taught carefully. If two or three work groups are established in a class, instruction and monitoring will be simpler if seatwork assignments are planned so that there is a basic assignment that all students do, with additional activities at appropriate levels for each group. Some of the instruction can then be with the whole class, while a smaller amount can be reserved for each group.

When using differentiated assignments, adjustments in the grading system should be made so that lower-ability students can attain satisfactory grades.

Problem B

If she is not already doing so, Ms. Porter should be sure that she is spending adequate class time explaining the material to the whole class. This is preferable to trying to impart the instruction to individuals during seatwork. To avoid long presentations and the attendant problem of maintaining student attention and participation, divide the presentation into two (or more) segments, with short periods of seatwork or classwork in between.

Frequent work samples, written as well as oral, should be obtained from students during content development activities in order to keep abreast of student understanding.

Every student should be included in discussions or recitations in order to keep them involved in the activity.

Providing structure for classwork and homework is essential. All assignments in class should be begun as a group exercise. Dittos or worksheets that lead students through tasks in a step-by-step fashion with frequent, short written responses also are helpful.

Daily grades should be emphasized, and students should be provided with frequent feedback about their progress in order to support and encourage their efforts.

Problem C

Mr. Oliver should reconsider his classroom rules and procedures to determine whether they cover the misbehaviors that are causing him a problem. If adjustments are needed, the relevant rule or procedure should be restated and introduced to the students again. Mr. Oliver should also consider whether his monitoring is adequate or whether students are getting away with too much misbehavior before he deals with the problem. In addition, some measures to correct or prevent specific problems described in the case study are listed below.

Mr. Oliver may be overrelying on the "fine" system to respond to misbehavior. If so, it would be better to use such penalties only for a limited number of situations (for example, forgetting materials or disturbing the class). Recording fines can be simplified by keeping a clipboard with a list of students' names and a place for a daily record.

Compliance with procedures can be rewarded by awarding points toward grades. Give students daily points or checks for having appropriate materials, being in their seats and ready to work when the bell rings, and staying on task throughout the period.

There are several ways to help students remember to bring materials. A supply of pens or pencils may be kept on hand for emergency loans, with some penalty imposed when students have to borrow supplies. Students can be allowed to leave pencils and papers in the classroom so that they will always be available. These can be labeled or kept in a folder with the students' names and class period listed on it. If different materials are needed on different days, Mr. Oliver could have students keep a record of materials and assignments needed for the class so that they can refer to it as necessary. He could also post a list of books and other materials above or next to the door so that students could see it before they enter the room.

Before content presentations Mr. Oliver might remind students that he will call on them to answer and that they should not call out except when he signals that it is appropriate.

Inappropriate behavior during presentations should be stopped by a simple procedure, such as reminding students of the procedure or rule, without interfering with the flow of the lesson. If the behavior persists, a penalty can be imposed.

It is always helpful to move around the room during presentations and while students are engaged in seatwork activities. Mr. Oliver should walk by every student in the room, looking at papers to be sure that students are working on the right assignment and doing it correctly. He should avoid staying too long with any one student, and if a student needs additional help, he or she can come to a table or desk where Mr. Oliver can monitor all the students. Frequent circulating will tend to discourage note writers and talkers.

Chapter Nine
Case Study 9-1

Diagnosis.   Mr. Davis has failed to be specific with his students about his expectations for their behavior. His only rule is too general to serve for all situations. Because he used one general rule, Mr. Davis must constantly interpret concrete instances of infractions as they relate to the rule. Furthermore, he has not been specific about consequences and has mentioned only one penalty, that of going to the office. Mild misbehaviors at the beginning of the year have now escalated into more serious misbehaviors as students test the limits. At this stage Mr. Davis is receiving poor cooperation both in obtaining written work from students and in the area of class participation.

Suggestions.   Mr. Davis might begin to establish better behavior in his class in the following ways.

Reevaluate the rules and procedures with the intent of making them more specific, and introduce rules and procedures for areas that were previously not covered.

Select a time such as a Monday or the day after a vacation period to reintroduce and explain the rules and procedures, providing students with rationales for the desired behaviors and eliciting their cooperation in following them.

Review procedures for participating in class discussions and for those times when whispering and working together is allowed and when it is not.

Once the rules and procedures are introduced, clear and specific consequences for infractions should be stated. These should be tied to the behaviors themselves; trips to the office should be used only for the most serious offenses. Positive as well as negative consequences should be considered and communicated to students.

Monitor the class constantly with the goal of anticipating and preventing misbehavior before it occurs and noting appropriate behavior.

Make sure that students have enough work to do and that they understand it and are able to complete it. Require student attention during presentations and allow only relevant materials and books to be out on desks. Have students take notes during important parts of the presentation: Be explicit and teach them how to take notes. Require these as part of a notebook.

Break longer activities into shorter ones and vary the sequencing and routine for the sixth-period class. Students are tired at this time of the day and maintaining attention is not easy even with well-behaved classes.

Pace students through their work with statements such as, "You should be halfway through with this assignment by now," or "We will check the first part of the assignment in five minutes."

Reward academic performance and other desirable classroom behavior regularly. For students of this age, extra-credit points or privileges may be more reinforcing than public praise.

Case Study 9-2

Diagnosis.   Ms. Woods has problems keeping her general mathematics students responsible for their work assignments. In her alegbra classes, where students are more motivated, Ms. Woods has fewer problems. Her general mathematics students, however, may need help in learning to assemble a notebook, becoming responsible for doing quality work, and for completing it. Because 75 percent of their grade is based on tests, and because their daily work is checked only once a week, students probably think that their daily work is not very important. This has likely contributed to their poor sense of responsibility.

Suggestions.   Ms. Woods should review her accountability procedures and her grading system, giving consideration to the following items.

Make certain all students know how each assignment contributes to their overall grade and that instructions are clear with respect to completeness, neatness, quality of work, and due dates.

Monitor student progress frequently once standards have been established and students understand them. Students should receive regular feedback.

Check notebooks periodically for completeness, thus keeping students from getting too far behind.

Be explicit about what is to be included in the notebooks and how it should be organized. Notebooks should also contain a table of contents and a list of required assignments. Displaying a model notebook would be helpful.

Allow students to check their own assignments or to exchange papers. This will help provide immediate feedback, and it will allow for more frequent checking of required work.

Have students keep track of their daily grades, quizzes, and extra-credit work. Spend some class time helping them compute averages on different occasions during the grading period.

As students work, circulate and monitor student progress rather than remaining at the teacher's desk.

Check early with students who fail to turn in assignments. If students need help, provide it; otherwise, require that assignments be completed.

Do a small part of each assignment orally and question students to check for understanding.

Case Study 9-3

Diagnosis.   Ms. Grant has made a common mistake. She assumes that students will be able to follow her directions with a minimum of structuring or explanation on her part. In this case study she assigns lab work that requires students to work in groups but does not prepare them for this activity. Group assignments are handed out but not explained clearly, nor do students attend to the directions. When students move to their groups, transitions are disorderly, and once in the groups, directions are vague as to how students are to pursue the question, "What is in the box?". The activity drags, and several groups sit in dead time while others finish. Groups are expected to report their findings, but no directions are given about how to do this. At the end of the activity, Ms. Grant provides no wrap-up or evaluation, and she assigns a textbook reading on a different topic.

Suggestions.   Ms. Grant might achieve more success with her class if she presents information systematically. The following items will help.

State major goals and objectives and let students know what they will be responsible for knowing.

Call for attention and do not proceed without it. Require that students listen to directions and presentations. Have them respond to questions and demonstrations.

Explain precisely what behaviors are expected when students work together in groups on an assignment. At the same time, groups should pick a recorder who will be responsible for presenting the group reports to the rest of the class.

As groups are working, monitor and circulate to make certain they are on the right track. If widespread problems seem to be occurring, reteach the material. Allow students to begin work only when satisfied that they can complete the tasks satisfactorily.

Provide additional activities for groups who finish early so that unnecessary dead time is avoided.

Constructively evaluate the individual reports rather than accepting poor or incomplete answers.

Follow up the group activity with relevant discussion and a summary of the lesson.

Index